To Barbara
Enjoy cooking
w/ Love!
1/6/17

The Jambo Café Cookbook

Recipes and remembrances of my journey from Africa to America

Chef Ahmed M. Obo

The Jambo Café Cookbook

Recipes and Remembrances of My Journey from Africa to America

Chef Ahmed M. Obo

Copyright© 2015–2016 Ahmed M. Obo, All rights reserved.

Photography© 2015 as follows:

Ahmed M. Obo, 13, 14, 15, 16, 20, 21, 44, 73
Lyn Avery, 9, 10, 11, 12, 28, 29, 38, 39, 78, 84, 124, 146, 160
Bob Gale, 10 (map)
Kitty Leaken, Cover, 32, 41, 43, 44
Lyric Kali, 57
Jane Phillips, 116, 121
Richard K. White, 26, 27, 37, 46, 50, 56, 58, 62, 64, 66, 70, 72, 76, 81,
    86, 90, 96, 100, 104, 108, 112, 122, 126, 130, 132, 136, 158

All rights reserved. Except as permitted under the U.S. Copyright Act of 1976, no part of this publication may be reproduced, distributed, or transmitted in any form or by any means, or stored in a data base or retrieval system, without prior written permission of the publisher.

First edition: March 2016

Limit of Liability/Disclaimer of Warranty: While the publisher/author has used his best efforts in preparing this book, he makes no representations or warranties with respect to the accuracy or completeness of the contents of this book and specifically disclaim any implied warranties of merchantability or fitness for a particular purpose. The publisher/author shall not be liable for any loss of profit or any other commercial damages, including but not limited to special incidental, consequential, or other damages.

Executive Editor: Lyric Kali

Editor and Narrative Writer: Janet Gotkin
Test Cook and Recipe Writer: Lyric Kali
Copyeditor: Alma B. Hall

Food Image Design: Lyric Kali, 26, 27, 37, 46, 50, 56, 58, 62, 64, 66, 70, 72, 76, 81, 86,
    90, 96, 100, 104, 108, 112, 122, 126, 130, 132, 136, 146

Book Design: John Cavanagh, 606 Design Co.

Orders by U.S. trade bookstores and wholesalers. Please contact Jambo Cafe at jambocafesf@gmail.com.

Printed in the United States of America

ISBN: 978-0-692-56554-4
Cooking

DEDICATION

For Paul Gotkin, 1942–2015, who first had the idea for this book and encouraged me to write it and to tell my story and Jambo's story. Paul didn't live to see this book completed, but his spirit is always with us.

And for my children, Mima and Salimu, who now know a little more about their Lamu family and their Swahili heritage.

ACKNOWLEDGEMENTS

This book was a long time coming and I couldn't have done it alone.

My deepest thanks to Lyric Kali, who revived this project when it was stalled and it looked as if it might never really come to be, testing (and re-retesting) all of the recipes until they were perfect, keeping us focused and energized, and guiding and overseeing every aspect of the editing, production, and design.

And thanks to the following people:

Janet Gotkin, who took on the task of helping me translate my life story and the story of my food, into a book.

Janet Bailey and Don Barliant, who have encouraged me in all my projects, and who early on provided a quick course in publishing, helping me decide what direction to take in producing this book.

All of the chefs who recognized my potential, and mentored me since I first came to the United States, opening the way for me to become the chef I am today.

The loyal, hardworking, supportive and always enthusiastic staff at Jambo Café. You are the best.

Lyn and Jim Avery, for urging me to follow my dreams, and for generously sharing Lyn's astoundingly beautiful photographs from Lamu.

My mother, for the love she bestowed on all of us and for the wonderful legacy of delicious food, which continues to inspire me every day.

My dad, who taught me the importance of working hard and not giving up.

My family in Lamu, Denver, and Santa Fe, who are always there for me.

My many friends and loyal customers, who have been asking me to create this cookbook since Jambo Café began, and who provide an unbreakable network of support, love, and inspiration.

My wife, Zuwena, who continues to give me love and encouragement.

My friend and American father, Paul Gotkin. This book was his 'baby' and all who knew and loved him are thrilled beyond words that *The Jambo Café Cookbook* has finally become a reality.

And to the Almighty for all the blessings You have given me.

CONTENTS

Introduction 9

Chapter 1: My Culinary Journey 13

Chapter 2: In Halima's Kitchen 15

Chapter 3: Spices for Life 29

Chapter 4: The Road to Jambo Cafe 39

Chapter 5: Soups 45

Chapter 6: Small Plates 55

Chapter 7: Chutneys and Sauces 69

Chapter 8: Sides 79

Chapter 9: Stews 85

Chapter 10: Meat 99

Chapter 11: Fish 111

Chapter 12: Sweets 125

Chapter 13: Drinks 135

Glossary 140

Where to Find It 147

Index 148

INTRODUCTION

When I was little my grandfather used to tell me about the time he had signed on to a cargo *dhow* that, with its load of turtle shells and mangrove poles, was heading down the East coast of Africa to Zanzibar and then out across the Indian Ocean to Oman, India, and Ceylon. He said the *dhow* was over eighty feet long and weighed nearly two hundred tons. It carried a crew of twenty-five men, whose job it was to raise and lower the huge triangular *lateen* sail that had to be swung across the deck whenever the wind switched direction. It was the kind of voyage East Africans had been making for well over a thousand years, sailing with the monsoon winds that blow south to north in the summer and north to south in the winter.

What my grandfather wanted to communicate when he told me stories about his adventures was that our lives have always been tied up with the sea.

My family is *Bajun*. We speak Swahili, sometimes called Kiswahili. Swahili means coastal people and it is a non-tribal language spoken widely across East Africa. My grandparents grew up in Kiunga, a tiny village in the northeast corner of Kenya, where, for generations, people had earned their keep by farming and fishing. The village was right

across the border from Somalia, and in the 1960s, with the government collapsing and bandits running free, Somalia had become a very dangerous place. Along with many other people, my family moved fifty miles down the coast to Lamu Island, which is where I was born.

Lamu is an extraordinary place. It was designated a World Heritage Site by UNESCO in 1993. Along with Zanzibar, it is what is left of the great Swahili city-states that sprang up along the East coast of Africa in the eleventh and twelfth centuries. Starting out as tiny trading posts, these settlements grew into huge independent kingdoms that stretched from Ged in Mozambique to Mogadishu in Somalia. They were great stone and coral cities, with cobblestone streets, a sophisticated sewer system, glittering round-domed mosques (Islam took hold along the coast around 1200) and even palaces like Husuni Kubwa, an enormous complex in Kilwa, Tanzania.

In their heyday, from the eleventh to the fourteenth century, these Swahili trading states grew enormously wealthy, shipping ivory, gold,

rhino horns, timber, ebony and ambergris to the Middle and the Far East. In 1414, the Kingdom of Malindi even sent two giraffes across the ocean as a gift to Yung-lo, the emperor of China. The kingdoms began to decline in the middle of the fifteenth century when a Portuguese fleet sailed around the Cape of Good Hope and set out to systematically conquer the coast, which turned out to be easier than they expected, since the Swahili states had never united.

At the height of its power, Swahili society was diverse, multi-ethnic and culturally complex. Swahilis are the ultimate fusion people, a mixture of sub-Saharan Africans, Arabs, Persians and Indians. Some of the most prominent Swahili families have Arab surnames and trace their lineage back to the Middle East. This cultural mix is seen in all parts of present day Swahili life, in the brightly colored *kangas* or cotton shawls Kenyan women wear, in the Persian-style carved wooden doors throughout Lamu Old Town and, most particularly, in the cuisine, which is a mélange of African, Indian and Middle Eastern cooking.

Marcus Samuelsson, the world-renowned Ethiopian-born chef, has written that "to understand African cooking you have to understand Africa." That is especially true of Swahili cooking, which is intertwined with the history of the Swahili people. The foods my mother cooked over a charcoal brazier—*ugali*, coconut rice, *pili pili*—all have their roots in far-flung places.

Swahili cuisine continues to evolve, but the most creative and memorable dishes are not necessarily found in the seaside restaurants, but in the kitchens of the inventive people who create new versions of traditional recipes to feed their families as well as the tourists who come to

experience the unique culture of Lamu. Lucky visitors might very well be met at the seaside by a man who offers to cook a meal for them in his home, giving them an opportunity to taste the best that Lamu has to offer.

In developing recipes for Jambo Café as well as new recipes specifically for this book, I have drawn on many culinary traditions, but the most profound and enduring influence continues to be the food of my childhood. I have adapted recipes using Caribbean spices and fused North African and Indian flavor profiles into those traditional dishes, incorporating herbs and cooking methods that reflect many cultures.

Some Swahili-influenced recipes might not be recognizable to people in Lamu. Soups, for example, which are an American favorite, are not traditionally Swahili, but my soups, which are based on fragrant, intensely flavored *masalas*, are a tribute to the food of my Swahili homeland.

Words really can't communicate the essence of any cuisine. Only the food can do that. My goal for this cookbook is to allow American cooks to enter into the heart of the cuisine I have developed, which integrates East African, Caribbean, Indian, and North African flavors—and continues to embrace new influences—and give them the tools and recipes so they can experience it for themselves.

MY CULINARY JOURNEY 1

On a snowy, bitter cold night in February 1995 I stepped off a jumbo jet at New York's JFK Airport. I had only a vague idea of what I was going to be doing in America. I certainly couldn't ever have imagined that only a decade and a half later I would be chef/owner of an immensely popular restaurant in food-obsessed Santa Fe, New Mexico. That idea would have struck me as ludicrous. I was a relatively uneducated twenty-two year old, an African from a tiny island called Lamu off the coast of Kenya, with only the basic cooking skills I had learned preparing fresh fish for tourists when I took them out on my family's *dhow,* a single-sailed, traditional, East African boat.

My American cultural and culinary journey started in New York. I was taught and mentored by the chef at a fine restaurant called The Fish Cellar, where I worked for almost two years. In New York, and later in Santa Fe, I tasted cuisines I had never been exposed to before—Chinese, Italian, Jewish (bagels and lox, gefilte fish), and American "diner" food.

Returning to Santa Fe after two years in New York, I worked at a fine restaurant in a boutique hotel, at a Middle Eastern restaurant that served falafel, and then at the Zia Diner, where I was Executive Chef for ten years. I honed my skills and broadened my tastes, experiencing a wide variety of foods both in professional kitchens and sharing meals with friends from around the globe. Finally, in August 2009 I opened Jambo Café.

In one sense, this cookbook is the story of my rather incredible journey, told through the meals I grew up with and the recipes I now prepare. But there is a mystery at the heart of this book, something I continue to wonder about. I grew up poor, the eldest of ten children. The meals my mother prepared for us were spare, cooked on charcoal braziers or over an open fire. Even in my late teens, when I earned enough to support my family, I had virtually no contact with fine cuisine. And yet, when I sat down to devise a menu for the African restaurant I planned to open, ideas kept pouring out of me, as if from some secret wellspring I had no idea was there.

After fifteen years in American kitchens, I had gathered a great deal of culinary knowledge, confidence and skill. But where in the world did the sophisticated combination of flavors I was creating come from—what one critic described as "sweet and tangy, fiery and subtle?" Best as I could figure, this knowledge was deeply woven into who I was.

Swahili cooking has been continuously evolving for a thousand years, influenced by the many cultures that make up the Swahili people—African, Arab, Persian, Berber, Chinese, and Portuguese. The most interesting food, however, is not being produced by five-star chefs in stainless steel kitchens. Creativity, I realize now, had been flourishing all around me, all my life, in my mom's simple kitchen, in the homes of my *shangazis* (aunts), in the food stalls where I first sampled Swahili *samosas* and *mishkaki* (skewers) and *vitumbuas* (coconut cakes).

Masalas, spice mixtures that each cook laboriously grinds and blends by hand, form the essence of Swahili food. Recently, on a trip back home, I wandered through an open-air market in Lamu, checking out the fresh fruits and vegetables and the straw baskets brimming with dried beans, rice, cumin seeds, ginger roots, cayenne peppers, cinnamon sticks and turmeric. I watched my sister as she made from scratch the naan-like breads called roti and chapatti that are a standard part of a Swahili meal. I was reminded again how much of my cooking was rooted in the everyday life of my family and friends. Even today, in the foods I prepare which reflect many cultures, spice mixtures form the foundation.

And so, as you try out my recipes—both traditional Swahili dishes and my own, new versions of these staples, as well as dishes that draw on culinary traditions from places as far from East Africa as the Caribbean and the Middle East—please remember that this food, like the food I grew up on, is essentially ordinary people's food. These dishes may seem sophisticated and complex, but as you prepare them in your kitchen, you will see they follow an ages old pattern—simple ingredients, fragrant, bold spice mixtures, and easy-to-duplicate cooking methods. You will be taking part, just as I did, in a culinary voyage from the ancient Swahili coast of Africa to the dry, beautiful Land of Enchantment that is New Mexico in 2015.

IN HALIMA'S KITCHEN 2

Like most people, I took the food I ate as a child for granted. Looking back now, I can see how much my childhood influenced my cooking. I was fortunate to be born on Lamu Island, in what has been called "the cradle of Swahili civilization." My father, Mohammed, and my mother, Halima, were refugees, having relocated when they were in their teens, from a tiny village less than ten miles from the Somali border. My ancestors were farmers and fishermen and I often think about how different my life might have been if I hadn't been brought up in busy, bustling, vibrant Lamu.

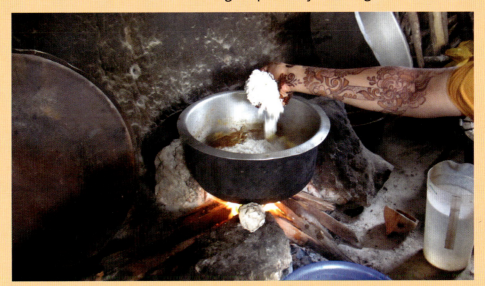

It wasn't until I was in my teens that I realized how hard life was for my parents. I was too much in love with the dhows that sailed around Lamu Bay and with the crowds of tourists who strolled along the ancient sea front. Swahili culture stretches back a thousand years, as does its constantly evolving cuisine, which has been influenced by the many different people who traded with the city-states that once spread across the whole East coast of Africa. Swahili cooking techniques allowed poor women like my mother, with a husband, in-laws, and many children to feed, to coax extraordinary flavor out of the simplest ingredients. She was a skilled and inventive cook and she has influenced my cooking more than anyone else in my life.

At night, my mother began to prepare the meal for the following day, mixing together the ingredients for the dense savory bread called *Mkate wa Nazi*. It was made with corn meal and shredded coconut. Corn was first introduced into Kenya in the late nineteenth century and it has replaced sorghum and millet as the cheapest and most abundant grain. Early in the morning, my mother would light the fuel in the charcoal-burning metal cooking stove called a *jiko*, or, sometimes, in a wood-fueled three-stone stove, and begin to bake her discs of bread. Before I went to school I would sell these discs in the marketplace and my mother would deliver some of her bread to local restaurants. This is how we paid for the rest of the day's meals.

By any standards we were poor, living in a succession of small, rented houses that often sheltered my mother, father, me and my nine brothers and sisters, as well as numerous cousins, aunts, and in-laws. Often, milky chai made with black tea and fragrant, coconut-infused bread, was all we had for breakfast. Eggs and dairy were never part of our diets, although I remember there was always milk in the house, delivered each morning in large jars, ready to be boiled so that it was safe for the many babies in our home.

Lunch was the main meal of the day. Sitting on mats on the floor, we shared a mountain of rice or *ugali*, always prepared with coconut, garlic, salt, and spices like cardamom or turmeric, and sometimes supplemented by bananas or mangoes, which grew plentifully in Lamu. When we had protein—and often we didn't—it was usually fish, which was plentiful and relatively inexpensive. My mother would carefully divide

IN HALIMA'S KITCHEN 2

the protein into small portions so that everyone had a piece. We ate a lot of beans, which were available at the market where my mother purchased rice and the many spices she used to make pungent sauces. Occasionally we had greens like spinach and very rarely a treat like chicken, which my mother cooked into a delicious, spicy, coconut-based curry.

Until a British veterinarian obtained a grant and instituted a system to neuter the cats on Lamu, our island was famous for the number of cats who circulated among all the houses and restaurants. They weren't pets in the Western sense, although each family had one or several cats. They were always hungry and if we weren't careful we would end up sharing our small protein portion with a determined cat.

Our diet was 99% carbohydrate and 1% protein but my memory is that our food was always shared with family and made tasty by my mother's constant efforts in her small kitchen.

All through my childhood I watched my mother—and later my sisters—as they cooked, preparing rice, *ugali*, and breads, grilling fish, and making complicated sauces that transformed simple ingredients into filling, satisfying meals for large numbers of people. After school I and my brothers and sisters helped my mother prepare our lunch, grating coconut and mixing spices, but it wasn't until I started going out on our *dhow* with my father that I learned to dry and grill fish. Later, when I moved to a small apartment and began taking tourists out on overnight dhow trips, I began to cook on my own for the first time, experimenting with spice mixtures and asking my mother and sisters for cooking advice.

When I came to the United States, I brought only simple cooking skills, but I carried with me the memories of the food of my childhood. The smells were delicious: coconut bread baking in the early morning, spices adding sweetness to the air, or sauces simmering, ready to be added to rice or fish. My family gathered together to share the meals that were prepared by my mother, who was determined that we would be nourished and fed, even when times were difficult and money was scarce. Food, caring, family. These are the enduring memories I have of Halima's kitchen.

MKATE WA NAZI OR RICE CAKES

Prep Time: 15 minutes
Cook Time: 15 minutes
Yield: 12–16 cakes.

Ingredients:
½ cup rice flour or a gluten-free rice flour blend
½ cup white corn meal
½ cup unsweetened shredded coconut
2 teaspoons dried coriander
¼ teaspoon baking powder*
1 tablespoon sugar
1 small red or yellow onion, diced fine
½ cup coconut milk
Oil for cooking

In a medium-sized bowl whisk all dry ingredients together. Stir in the coconut milk to create a thick batter. Heat a griddle or skillet over medium high heat, brush the surface with a bit of olive oil, and place a tablespoon-sized dollop of batter in the pan. Cook for 60–75 seconds and flip to the other side. Flatten the cake with a spatula and cook for an additional 60–75 seconds until the cake is golden brown and cooked through. Serve hot or warm with a bit of honey, maple syrup or other topping as desired.

*Amount for high altitude cooking of 3,000 or more feet above sea-level. If cooking at low altitude increase your leavening agent to ½ teaspoon.

IN HALIMA'S KITCHEN 2

MKATE WA MUFA OR CORN MEAL BREAD

Prep Time: 30 minutes
Cook Time: 20–30 minutes
Serves: 4–6

Ingredients:
1½ cups white corn meal
½ cup flour
½ teaspoon salt
1 teaspoon sugar
1 small red onion, grated
1 teaspoon yeast
1 cup water
1 cup vegetable oil for frying

Put the corn meal, flour, salt, sugar, onions, and yeast in a large bowl and mix with your hands. Add water as needed until the dough feels sticky. Cover with a clean dish cloth and let sit for 15 minutes.

Form the mixture into patties about the size of the palm of your hand and set aside on a plate.

Add oil to a medium-sized frying pan and cook over medium-high heat until the oil is hot, 365 to 375 degrees. Fry the patties, in batches, to a golden brown. Drain on paper towels. Serve hot with honey, butter, or your choice of jam or preserves.

HALIMA MAKING MKATE WA NAZI IN THE TRADITIONAL MANNER

1. Ahmed's mom, Halima and a banana leaf, parts of which will act as a mold for the Mkate Wa Nazi.

2. A length of banana leaf to be shaped into the mold

3. Folding over the end to form a triangle-shaped pocket

4. Folding over the final side and securing with a toothpick

5. Getting ready to crack a coconut, a refreshing staple

6. Shredded coconut in the raw

IN HALIMA'S KITCHEN 2

7. Mixing in the rice flour, corn meal, leavening agent, and onions

8. A Jiko stove, a charcoal-based stove used by many in Kenya as an alternative to wood fire cooking

9. Mkate Wa Nazi in their banana leaf packets placed on the Jiko stove

10. The banana leaves will char as the Mkate Wa Nazi cooks; turn over the packets midway through.

11. Remove the Mkate Wa Nazi cakes from the banana leaves once they cook to firm. Brown a bit more as desired.

12. A toasted Mkate Wa Nazi ready to eat!

UGALI

Ugali is a traditional dish made from cornmeal, millet, or sorghum flour mixed with water

Prep Time: 5 minutes
Cook Time: 10 minutes
Serves: 4–6

Ingredients:
4 cups water
Salt
2 cups white corn meal

Bring a large pot of salted water to a boil. Turn heat to low and remove ½ cup of water in a liquid measuring cup and reserve. Add the corn meal slowly, stirring constantly with a wooden spoon. As you add the corn meal to the water the mixture will thicken until it feels like a paste and doesn't stick to the pot. If the mixture is hard, then add a bit of reserved water. Continue to stir the mixture until the ugali comes up easily out of the pot. Serve with any stew or dish with a sauce.

IN HALIMA'S KITCHEN 2

CASSAVA AND PLANTAIN FUFU

Fufu is a dough made from boiled or ground plantain or cassava and is a dietary staple in many parts of Africa.

Prep Time: 20–30 minutes
Cook Time: 30–45 minutes
Serves: 4–6

Ingredients:
2 medium cassava (yuca root or manioc)
2 plantains, yellow with a bit of brown spotting but not too soft
Salt and freshly cracked black pepper to taste
2 tablespoons butter (add more to taste)

To peel the Cassava see page 66 for pictorial instructions.

Bring salted water to boil in a large pot. Add the cassava pieces and boil until soft, about 30 minutes.

While the cassava is boiling, peel the plantains and dice them. In a medium pot bring salted water to boil and boil the plantains for about 15 minutes to soften them.

Drain the cassava and let cool slightly in order to pull the center core out of the cassava. Discard the core. Place the cassava in a large bowl.

Drain the plantains and add them to the bowl with the cassava. Add butter while mashing with a wooden spoon. Add salt and pepper to taste.

Serve warm with any stew.

ROTI

Roti is an East African bread like the Indian Naan, typically served with chai for an afternoon snack or with stews.

Prep Time: 40 minutes
Cook Time: 20 minutes
Serves: 4

Ingredients:
2 cups all purpose flour
4-5 green onions, green part only, chopped
1 teaspoon salt
1 cup unsalted butter, melted
1 cup warm water, more as needed

Place flour, scallions, and salt into a large bowl and mix with your hands. Add ¼ cup melted butter slowly while mixing gently; the mixture will begin to resemble a coarse cornmeal. Pour in the warm water slowly as you vigorously mix the ingredients with your fingers until a dough forms. The dough should not be sticky; if it is add a bit more flour.

(See step-by-step pictorial on page 26) Separate the dough into 4 balls; eventually each one of these balls will be a roti. Place the dough balls on a plate so that they don't touch each other. Cover with a larger bowl for 10 minutes.

Put a little flour on a clean cutting board or counter and roll one of the dough balls out with a floured rolling pin. The rolled out dough should measure 7–8 inches in length. Using a pastry brush, brush on some melted butter.

IN HALIMA'S KITCHEN   2

From the edge nearest to you, roll the dough away from you. Stretch it and then turn the dough clockwise one quarter turn; then again roll the dough away from you. Tuck the ends in. The dough should now feel thicker and more dense. With the palm of your hand squash the dough bundle, turn it clockwise one quarter turn and squash it again with the palm of your hand. With a rolling pin, roll the dough to a 7–8 inch round. If the dough sticks to the work surface or the rolling pin, add a bit of flour. Repeat with the remaining 3 dough balls. You now have 4 rotis ready to cook.

Heat a 10-inch nonstick pan on medium heat and add some butter to the pan.

Brush a roti with melted butter and place butter side down in the pan. With a spatula press down on the roti and cook for 1–2 minutes. Flip the roti and brush on more butter, cooking for an additional 1–2 minutes. Flip the roti and repeat. Flip the roti again and repeat. You will flip the roti three times in total, cooking each side of the roti twice. The roti should have spots of golden brown on both sides. Repeat the process with the other dough balls.

Serve hot with chai or as a side dish to a curry, stew, or soup.

MAKING ROTI

1. With a rolling pin, roll one roti ball to a 7–8" diameter round.

2. Fold over in 1" folds away from you.

3. The roti should fold about 7 times.

4. And should result in a thin strip of dough.

5. Roll it into a spiral from one end.

6. Once rolled it should look similar to a cinnamon bun.

IN HALIMA'S KITCHEN 2

7. Lay the roll flat and squash it with the palm of your hand.

8. Roll it out again with your rolling pin. You'll notice the dough is stiffer and harder to roll.

9. Keep rolling it out to a 7–8" diameter

10. Your roti should be flat and thin. Repeat with all other roti balls.

11. Cook it up according to directions and serve with chai or a sauce of your choice

12. Take a break and enjoy!

JAMBO CAFE 27

SPICES FOR LIFE 3

As a boy in Lamu I would take the few shillings my mother gave me in the morning before I went to school and walk to the market to buy the spices that she needed to prepare the main meal of the day. She didn't call them "spices," though. There really is no Swahili word for spices. The word we use is *dawa*, which actually means medicines. Or *madawa*, which means a mixture of several spices or medicines. When my mother or sisters cooked, they added the brilliant flavors of cumin, ginger, cardamom, or turmeric (*madawa*) to the sauces, called *mchuzi*, that they made for the rice, *ugali*, or chicken; these *madawa* were a kind of medicine for the *mchuzi*, giving them flavor, intensity, and life.

When I walked to the market in Lamu I saw vendors who spread out boxes and bags of ground spices—cumin, ginger, cayenne, turmeric, or cardamom—and cinnamon and nutmeg, especially for tea. The sellers would measure and weigh small amounts of spices, just what I needed if I said my mother was making a chicken curry or grilled fish for our lunch. Specialized vendors sold spice and herb mixtures in small packets, already made up, or whole spices like allspice, fennel, caraway seeds or cloves.

In cultures all over the world spices add life to food, but on the East coast of Africa spices are so central to our cooking that it isn't possible to imagine our food without them. The spices that influence our cooking come from many places—Africa, the Middle East, and India. They arrived on the Swahili coast after the Portuguese invaded in the late 1400s, conquering Lamu and making it a central hub for trade across the Indian Ocean. Following the path of the monsoons, traders brought silks, porcelains and spices from Zanzibar, Arabia and the Indian sub-continent.

When I was a child I would walk along the seafront in Lamu where I could see the ships and *dhows* arrive. I would watch as the sacks of spices were unloaded, ready to make their way into markets and stores. The aroma was heavenly, the same heady scent that filled our noses when we walked into our house after a morning at school, ready for lunch.

When I moved to New Mexico I encountered green and red chile for the first time. Our New Mexican chiles are different from the flavors I grew up with. But they were also familiar in their intensity and undertones, since I was used to cooking and eating hot, aromatic food. In Santa Fe I noticed that Indian restaurants were popular and the flavors in those restaurants reminded me of home. I realized that Americans were open to eating spicy, highly flavored food and I remember thinking that Santa Fe was a good place to cook my kind of food.

SPICES FOR LIFE 3

At the time, the mid 1990s, I was still new to America. I didn't realize it then, but Americans were embracing foods from all over the world—Mexico, Central America, the Caribbean, Korea, Vietnam, Thailand, and Ethiopia. Nowhere was that clearer than in Santa Fe, where residents and visitors alike wanted to sample exciting and exotic foods. And they still do. An article I read recently said that America had become "a nation of food fanatics" and it quoted numbers indicating that sales of salsa are outpacing ketchup.

Cooking with spices is like painting. In painting you add layers of color, allowing the most important colors to stand out, to sort of rise to the surface. In cooking you combine flavors and balance them, encouraging the spices to identify themselves. Balance is the secret. In the black bean and sweet potato soup I made for the Souper Bowl in Santa Fe, an annual fundraiser for The Food Depot, I had to counter the basic sweetness of the potatoes, add some earthiness from an herb like thyme, and balance the flavors, deciding if I wanted the cayenne or the ginger to prevail.

In Lamu we barely used herbs at all. In the U.S. I learned to experiment.

Herbs—green, leafy products like mint, rosemary and thyme—grow in the more temperate climates like Europe and were not available in Lamu when I was growing up. Spices—fragrant, aromatic plant products like cinnamon, cloves, ginger and pepper—grow in tropical and subtropical regions of the world and were part of the daily experience of food in East Africa. Today, around the world, the word "spice" has come to mean any dried plant product used in cooking for seasoning. It's a kind of all-purpose definition that covers a wide range of plants like herbs, spices, seeds, roots, bark, and even dehydrated vegetables and spice blends.

Spice mixtures called *masalas* are used in every Indian and Swahili kitchen and were part of my mother's cooking. *Masalas* are blends of dried spices; some blends, like *garam masala*, are world-famous. These spice blends make Indian and Swahili cuisine both unique and difficult to reproduce, since in Lamu and other places along the Swahili Coast, cooks rarely use measuring utensils.

Spice blends, often made into a paste, have formed a natural basis for my cooking, especially in soups and stews. The flavors and combinations have changed and evolved as I've added new ingredients and standardized the mixtures so that the cooks in the kitchen of Jambo Café, and the users of this book, can be confident that each and every time they make a recipe it will be successful.

I don't know if I really have 'favorite' spices or spices I absolutely could not cook without, but customers at Jambo Café and cooks buying spices at Jambo Imports ask me again and again which are the "can't do without" spices in my cooking. So, here they are: ginger, cayenne, coriander, cumin, and cinnamon, although I would have to add curry powder to that list, even though curry powder itself is a mixture of spices that can vary from place to place and cook to cook.

The history of spices in the Caribbean is similar to Lamu because the islands were part of the global spice trade. Authentic Caribbean cuisine represents all the cultural influences the Caribbean Islands have experienced since the late 15th century. It is spicy but healthy, using fruits and vegetables, and featuring unique spice mixtures, especially jerk spices, which originated in Jamaica.

It was eating at a friend's home in Santa Fe that I first experienced Caribbean food. I had been invited for dinner, and when I walked into the house for a moment I thought I was in Lamu—the same spicy, cinnamon-tinged, delicious smell. As I became more familiar with Caribbean cuisine and compared it to the Swahili food of my childhood, the similarities and differences became clearer. The biggest difference is the widespread use of allspice, and thyme

SPICES FOR LIFE 3

in Caribbean cooking. I fell in love with this layered, flavorful, comforting cuisine and knew I wanted to incorporate these flavors into my cooking.

I made some changes to the Caribbean recipes my friends used, altering cooking methods while keeping the unique spice combinations. An example is how I cook Jerk Chicken at Jambo. I started with a classic Caribbean Jerk Chicken recipe and decided to cook the chicken a little bit differently. After grilling it, I cook it slowly in the oven for a long time so that the meat becomes very tender, falling off the bones. It is still jerk chicken, it is still connected to its Caribbean roots, but it's also changed. This is how new cuisines develop.

When I began to plan the menu for the restaurant that would become Jambo Café I knew I wanted to expand the flavor profiles of the food I would offer, while continuing to emphasize my Swahili roots. I named it *Jambo*, which means "hello" in Swahili. That concept has evolved, and now you can see the influences of Caribbean and North African flavors at Jambo, and in the recipes in this book, and there will be even more variety in the future.

Certain childhood experiences are so special I believe I have tried to recreate them in my food and at Jambo. My favorite place to visit when I was younger was the island of Zanzibar. The moment you land the smell of cloves surrounds you. It is truly a blessed place. I have a lasting memory of going on a Spice Tour in Zanzibar, touring the clove plantations that once made Zanzibar the center of the world's clove trade. The memory of the lush green farms and the deep, spicy aroma of the cloves have stayed with me. I loved those smells and I still love them.

Today, when you walk into Jambo Café you are greeted by a heady, sweet and spicy aroma. It is like walking into my mother's kitchen in Lamu, trolling the seafront to watch the ships unload their spice cargoes, enjoying new foods like hummus and Jamaican jerk chicken with friends, or touring Zanzibar. It is old but it is also new; familiar, but different. And always, I hope, delicious.

BAHARAT SPICE BLEND

Prep Time: 10 minutes
Yields: approximately 1¼ cups

Ingredients:
2 tablespoons ground green cardamom
4 tablespoons smoked sweet paprika
4 tablespoons ground coriander
3 tablespoons ground cinnamon
3 tablespoons ground cumin
1 tablespoons black pepper
1 teaspoon ground cloves
½ tablespoon ground nutmeg

Green cardamom is best ground from the pods. In a mortar and pestle or a clean coffee grinder pulse green cardamom pods to a powder. About 35–40 pods will yield 2 tablespoons of powder. In a medium-sized bowl place all ground spices and mix well using a whisk or fork. Store in a glass jar in a cool dry place.

HARISSA SPICE BLEND

Prep Time: 10 minutes
Yields: approximately 1 cup

Ingredients:
1 tablespoon ground caraway seeds
5 African bird's eye chiles
4 tablespoons smoked sweet paprika

SPICES FOR LIFE

2 tablespoons ground cumin
2 tablespoons ground coriander
1 tablespoon red chile powder

In a mortar and pestle or a clean coffee grinder pulse the caraway seeds and chiles to a powder. In a medium-sized bowl combine the seeds and chiles and all ingredients mixing well with a whisk or fork. Store in a glass jar in a cool dry place.

RAS EL HANOUT SPICE BLEND

Prep Time: 10 minutes
Yields: approximately ½ cup

Ingredients:
3 tablespoons ground cinnamon
3 tablespoons ground turmeric
3 teaspoons ground allspice
1½ teaspoons ground nutmeg
1½ teaspoons saffron threads
3 teaspoons ground green cardamom
3 teaspoons ground thyme
3 teaspoons salt
3 teaspoons freshly ground black pepper

In a medium-sized bowl combine all ingredients and mix well with a whisk or fork. Store in a glass jar in a cool dry place.

PILI PILI SPICE PASTE

Prep Time: 10 minutes
Yields: approximately ¾ cup

Ingredients:
8–9 African bird's eye chiles
3 tablespoons ground coriander
3 tablespoons ground paprika
3–5 tablespoons ground cayenne, to taste
3 tablespoons kosher salt
1½ teaspoons crushed black pepper
3 tablespoons brown sugar
3 tablespoons fresh garlic, crushed
½ cup fresh lemon juice

In a mortar and pestle or clean coffee grinder pulse the chiles to a powder. In a medium-sized bowl combine all ingredients and mix well with a fork to create a paste. Store in a glass jar in the refrigerator for up to 2 weeks.

THE ROAD TO JAMBO CAFE 4

I've always loved to cook. I spent most of my adult life cooking for people or working in kitchens, but it wasn't until I had been in the United States for nearly twelve years that I let myself believe that I might someday join the ranks of American chef-restaurant owners.

In Lamu I took tourists out to fish on my *dhow*. Often, we stayed out overnight and I cooked simple dinners for them, usually grilling fresh fish that we had caught during the day. I remember more than one person saying, "You could open a restaurant with food like this," but I was very young, only a teen-ager, and opening a restaurant was as unreal to me as the thought of traveling to America. I was the oldest of my ten siblings and I was working to support my mother and family. I didn't have many thoughts about the future.

In the winter of 1995, newly married to an American woman I had met in Lamu, I arrived in New York. After a few months in New York, we settled in Santa Fe almost by accident; a friend from Lamu who was living and working in Santa Fe found us an apartment and got me a job in a small but busy restaurant called Atalaya. I had thought of doing something different in America, maybe working in construction, but I needed a job. Before I knew it I was cooking again, but in a very new environment, a commercial kitchen, where I prepared everything from salads to omelets, hummus, falafel, green chile cheese burgers, burritos and enchiladas.

Six months after my daughter was born, feeling homesick, we set out in our ancient Volkswagen, in the middle of January, aiming to stay for a short while in New York and then to take a long, leisurely visit to Lamu. After the car broke down in the middle of a blizzard in Cleveland, we arrived on a snowy night in Croton-on-Hudson, NY, to stay with my in-laws, Janet and Paul Gotkin, who had welcomed me to the United States when I had first arrived. We lived in New York for two years, where a fortunate job set me firmly on my professional culinary path.

I had never formally applied for a job before, but I answered an ad in a local paper for a cook at a new restaurant in Mt. Kisco, NY. I drove the back roads of Westchester County to The Fish Cellar, interviewed, and got the job.

The Fish Cellar was started by Joe DiMauro, who had owned a successful fish store for 30 years in a small, affluent community about 45 minutes north of New York City. He had hired a young chef, Joseph Sasso, and together they had a vision: to provide fresh, delicious fish dishes in a beautiful setting. And I was going to be part of this venture.

From the very beginning I watched and learned. The Swahili tradition is straightforward; fish is cooked thoroughly and completely, all at one time. The chef's approach was completely different. He partially cooked the fish, leaving it firm and moist; then he cooked the vegetables with herbs like basil, tarragon and garlic. He pureed the herbs for the sauce, adding them to the tender fish. It was delicious. Up to that moment, I had thought I knew all there was to know about cooking fish.

I worked at The Fish Cellar for nearly two years. Every new challenge was a chance to learn. The chef liked me and I liked him. He took me under his wing, teaching me basic and advanced cooking techniques, and nurturing my interest and talent. When the sous chef left, I became Joe's assistant. Joe shared his knowledge generously, always encouraging me to try new ingredients, new recipes, new ways of cooking. He respected me and he instilled respect. Quite simply, he taught me how to be a chef.

After two years in New York, we headed back to Santa Fe. I returned with skills and confidence. Quickly, I got a job at the 5-star restaurant at the downtown luxury boutique hotel, The Inn of the Anasazi, where I worked for a year. Again, I was fortunate to work for a chef who believed in me and, after a little while, he urged me to use my ideas and skills to create

THE ROAD TO JAMBO CAFE 4

my first dinner special. I believe it was trout; it was a huge success. In order to save money for a trip to Kenya, I took a part-time job as a line cook at the long-standing, popular Santa Fe institution, the Zia Diner, balancing two jobs until I headed to Lamu.

When I returned, Beth Koch, Zia's owner, offered me a full-time job. I had learned a lot since starting as a prep cook at Atalaya. Although I didn't have formal culinary education, I had worked under chefs who nurtured my abilities and set me on a course to becoming a professional chef. Still, nothing prepared me for how quickly my culinary path unfolded at the Zia, a path that would lead to the creation, in 2009, of Jambo Café.

This is how I became Executive Chef at the Zia Diner in six months.

I started as a line cook, working under the chef, Harold Orner. From the beginning, Harold offered me leeway in my cooking. He gave me responsibility to make the day's soups and specials, and urged me to create unusual dishes (unusual for Santa Fe, but not for Lamu) using spices like ginger and curry. At the Zia, under Harold, I made my first butternut squash ginger soup, and was surprised when customers called the restaurant to say how good it was.

Less than six months after I started at the Zia, the sous chef left suddenly; almost immediately after that, Harold left to help care for his ill father. In a flash, we were without leadership in the kitchen. Late in December of my first year, Beth called me into her office and offered me the job of Executive Chef.

I was shocked, thrilled, overwhelmed, and frightened. I didn't know if I could do the job. I had left school at age 12 to support my family and never returned. I had no formal culinary training. I would be doing inventory, ordering, supervising a kitchen with 16 people. Beth had shown her faith in me and given me a once-in-a-lifetime opportunity. With many doubts and misgivings, but the complete support of my family, I said yes. And I've never for a moment regretted it.

I stayed at the Zia for ten years, creating specials and soups and adding new dishes to the menu. I experimented with spices and herbs, even introducing some African-influenced specials, which were always popular. I learned to do ordering and inventory, and I faced the challenges of supervising a large staff in a busy kitchen, where tensions sometimes rose high. I will always be grateful to Beth at the Zia Diner, who offered me this extraordinary opportunity to advance in my career and to learn how to run a successful restaurant.

As I became restless, friends urged me to serve more African dishes at the Zia but I wanted to wait. I thought about starting a catering business or buying a food van. I almost did buy a food truck, but decided I wanted something more.

In 2009, one thing was becoming clear: I wanted to be my own boss and make the food I loved. I was ready to move on. Once I made the decision, I knew it was the right one. I had been Captain of my boat in Lamu, in charge of taking care of my family since I was a young teen-ager. I wanted to own my own restaurant and be the spark that would make a difference in the life of my family in Lamu.

TripAdvisor says that Santa Fe has more restaurants per capita than any other American city. Santa Feans do love to eat out and they are a demanding group. I ate a lot of delicious food during the years I worked at the Zia, but nothing matched the 'idea' I had in my head of the kind of food I wanted to serve and eat. Of course, what I wanted was food that reminded me of home, those coconut-infused, spice-laden stews and dishes my mother and sisters served up in our small home when I was a child.

With my father-in-law, Paul, I started to look at available restaurant spaces in Santa Fe. From the beginning, Paul was my biggest supporter. Even in the depths of the country's economic recession, when it didn't seem to make the best sense to start a new restaurant, he encouraged me and helped me believe I would be successful.

The space we found was perfect and a great value, although two previous restaurants had failed there. The kitchen was intact, and there was lots of parking and room to expand in the future. I signed a three and a half-year lease and started to work on developing the menu for my new

THE ROAD TO JAMBO CAFE 4

restaurant. There was no question about the name: it would be called Jambo Café. Jambo means 'hello' in Swahili and I was saying hello to Santa Fe: hello, come in, sample the food of my childhood and the food I'm making that is inspired by my childhood, and by all the new foods I've tasted and enjoyed and learned to cook—Caribbean, North African, Mediterranean, and more.

As I worked on the menu and the concept, I realized I had always had a dream of owning my own restaurant and cooking for people. My lifelong connection to food and to the Swahili culture had led me to this point. I was going to be able to make the food I loved, have a good life for myself and my American family, and help my family and my community in Lamu.

Friends, family, colleagues, and an amazing wait staff combined their efforts to launch Jambo Café in August of 2009 and help get us on our feet. Many of those wonderful servers and staff are still with me today. Gillian Labe, my friend and sous chef at the Zia, offered steady encouragement to open Jambo. Gillian continued to help, pitching in with other friends in the early weeks after I opened Jambo.

From the day it opened, Jambo Café was embraced by Santa Feans and, soon, by tourists coming to visit the city.

Ratings on online sites like TripAdvisor and Yelp were consistently high. In January of 2010, I entered Jambo Café in the Souper Bowl, Santa Fe's annual fundraiser for The Food Depot, a local food bank. I won Best Savory Soup and Best Soup in the competition, with a spiced coconut peanut chicken soup. In 2011 I won Best Vegetarian Soup and Best Soup overall with a curried black bean and sweet potato soup. In the 2012 Souper Bowl, Jambo's roasted butternut squash soup with crab captured the Best Seafood and Best Soup categories. In the 2013 competition, my spiced coconut cream guava-lime soup took the Best Cream and Best Soup prizes. These soups told the story of my culinary journey from Lamu to Santa Fe,

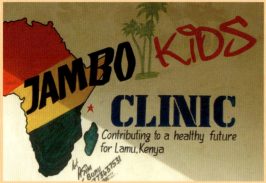

incorporating the flavors and techniques I had mastered with the help of chefs and mentors at The Fish Cellar, Inn of the Anasazi, and Zia Diner.

Santa Fe had embraced me and Jambo Café and its food. Without actually intending to, I was now making a new kind of cuisine, not really Swahili anymore, but a world cuisine with clear East African roots.

After a year and a half, Jambo expanded, doubling its space. From the moment the new part of the restaurant opened we have been busy greeting loyal guests and welcoming new ones.

America has truly been the land of opportunity for me. Here, you are judged by the food you produce, not by your credentials or the culinary school you attended. I became a 'chef,' not just a cook, because of my food.

Jambo Café's success has given me the freedom to do what I love in my own way, to cook and serve food to people, to encourage new chefs, and to give back to my Santa Fe community and my family and community in Lamu. I am thankful for the mentoring I've had along the way and the opportunities that were offered to me. I have personal success and financial security for my family in America and in Kenya.

I have been fortunate in many ways but none as great as in the love and encouragement I've experienced from my American family, Janet and Paul Gotkin, who embraced me as their son the day we first met on that cold, snowy day in February, 1995. Paul, especially, has been my father, my mentor, my advisor, my friend, and my supporter. Life without Paul is a challenge to all of us who loved him. I carry his love and the things he taught me deep in my heart.

I am grateful to the Almighty, who has embraced me in so many ways, with all the many blessings in my life: my mother and father, my brothers and sisters and family in Lamu, my children Mima and Salimu, dear friends, and, of course, my beloved wife, Zuwena.

Is Jambo Café the beginning or the end of my culinary journey? I'm busy with the restaurant, of course, and Jambo Imports store, and Jambo Kids Foundation and the clinic in Lamu. But, after the life I've lived so far, I am sure there will be new ventures and challenges ahead. Jambo Café is the beginning, not the end.

SOUPS

Soup is not part of traditional cooking in Lamu, although growing up we always had something savory at our meals, almost a kind of sauce, to complement the rice, *roti*, *ugali*, or *chapatti*. In American restaurants, soup is a staple of most menus. When I first started making soup I relied on my memories of the rich sauces my mother cooked to guide me, using spice mixtures as a starter. I enjoy experimenting and I use ingredients like beans, lentils, sweet potatoes and pumpkin, making everything from traditional stew-like soups, rich purees, bisques, and fruit and vegetable gazpachos.

CURRIED BLACK BEANS-SWEET POTATO WITH COCONUT CREAM

"Best Soup/Best Vegetarian Soup" in 2011 at Souper Bowl XVII

Prep Time: 15–20 minutes
Cook Time: 45–50 minutes
Serves: 4–6

Ingredients:
½ cup olive oil
1 small to medium yellow onion, chopped
2 tablespoons fresh ginger, grated
1 tablespoon garlic, minced
1½ tablespoons curry powder
1 tablespoon ground coriander
1 tablespoon ground cumin
½ tablespoon ground turmeric
1 tablespoon ground ginger
1 tablespoon dried thyme
2 tablespoons tomato paste
1 cup Roma tomatoes, diced
2 cups whole black beans, cooked
2 large sweet potatoes, peeled and diced
4 cups vegetable stock
1 can coconut cream (13.5 ounces)
2 tablespoons dry sherry wine
2 tablespoons rice wine vinegar
Salt to taste

Remember to cook the 2 cups of black beans before making this soup.

Over medium heat in a medium to large soup pot, heat the olive oil until shimmering. Add the onion, ginger and garlic and sauté 3–5 minutes until soft. Add the spices from the curry to thyme and cook for 2–3 minutes until the aroma of the spices pops. Add the tomato paste, mixing well for 1 minute. Add the Roma tomatoes and cook for 3 minutes until a paste forms. Stir in the black beans, sweet potatoes, and vegetable stock. Bring to a boil and reduce heat; simmer for 15–20 minutes until the vegetables are soft. Pour in the coconut milk, sherry wine, and rice wine vinegar. Stir well and add salt to taste. Cook for an additional 10–15 minutes on low to allow all the flavors to marry.

Turn off the stove and allow the soup to cool for 10 minutes. Using an immersion blender, puree the mixture to a creamy soup consistency. Add more stock as needed. If you don't have an immersion blender, puree the mixture in batches in your blender. Heat up the soup over medium heat for 5–10 minutes to serve hot.

ROASTED GINGER-BUTTERNUT SQUASH BISQUE

Prep Time: 30–45 minutes
Cook Time: 90 minutes
Serves: 4–6

Ingredients:
1 large butternut squash
½ pound butter
1 large yellow or red onion, diced
2 tablespoons fresh ginger, peeled and minced
½ tablespoon ground nutmeg
½ tablespoon ground allspice
½ tablespoon ground thyme
½ tablespoon ground coriander
5 cups vegetable stock
1 can coconut cream (13.5 ounces)
½ tablespoon salt

Preheat oven to 400 degrees. Cut the butternut squash in half and scoop out the seeds. Rub a little olive oil all over the squash halves and place flesh side down on a baking sheet. Roast in the oven for 45 minutes to 1 hour. When the skin is golden brown and soft, remove the squash from the oven and cool slightly. Peel the skin from the butternut squash and place the flesh in a large bowl and mash.

Melt the butter in a soup pot over low heat. Add the onion and ginger and cook on low until the onion is very soft, but not brown, about 10–12 minutes. Stir in the nutmeg, allspice, thyme, and coriander and cook on low for 2–3 minutes. Add the mashed butternut squash and cook on low for an additional 10 minutes. Pour in the vegetable stock and coconut cream and cook on low for an additional 15 minutes.

Remove from heat. With an immersion blender puree the soup or transfer the soup to a blender and puree in batches. Reheat the soup on low for 3–5 minutes and serve hot.

SWEET SMOKED PAPRIKA CORN AND SWEET POTATO SOUP

Prep Time: 30 minutes
Cook Time: 40 minutes
Serves: 4–6

Ingredients:
3 tablespoons olive oil
1 small yellow onion, diced small
1 tablespoon fresh garlic, minced
5 ribs celery, diced small
1 tablespoon sweet smoked paprika
1 tablespoon dried thyme
1 teaspoon Old Bay® Seasoning
¼ teaspoon cayenne
3 tablespoons tomato paste
2 medium sweet potatoes, peeled and diced small
4 ears sweet white corn, steamed, with kernels removed from the cob or 3 cups frozen sweet white corn kernels
4 cups vegetable stock
1 can coconut milk (13.5 ounces)
Salt and freshly ground black pepper to taste

Heat the olive oil over medium-high heat in a large saucepan or medium Dutch oven. Once the oil is shimmering, add the onions, garlic, and celery, sautéing for 5 minutes. Add the spices and cook, stirring for 3 minutes or until the spices start to stick to the pot. Add the tomato paste and stir for 1–2 minutes until thoroughly mixed. Add the sweet potato, stirring until well coated with spice mixture, cooking for an additional 3 minutes. Pour in the vegetable stock and coconut milk, mixing well, and bring to a boil. Reduce heat and simmer for 20 minutes or until the potatoes are tender.

Remove from heat. Using an immersion blender or a traditional blender, puree the sweet potato mixture until smooth. Return to heat, add the corn and salt and pepper, and cook for 3–5 minutes. If you wish to puree the entire soup mixture, add the corn during the last 5 minutes of simmer time, then puree. Serve hot.

MANGO GINGER GAZPACHO

Active Prep Time: 30 minutes
Inactive Prep Time: 6–12 hours
Serves: 4–6

Ingredients:
4 cups mango juice
2 small ripe mangoes, peeled, pitted, and diced
1 small red bell pepper, deseeded and diced
1 small cucumber, peeled, deseeded, and diced
1 cup juice from fresh ginger root
1 small jalapeño, deseeded and minced
1–2 green onions, green parts only, chopped fine
2 tablespoons fresh mint, chopped fine
Juice of one medium to large lemon, strained
½ teaspoon salt
Freshly cracked black pepper to taste
Dash of any hot sauce

Pour the mango juice into a large glass or ceramic bowl. Stir in the diced mangoes, red pepper, and cucumber.

Put the mangoes into a juicer in order to create 1 cup of juice. Stir into mango and vegetable mixture and add onions, jalapeño, mint, lemon, salt, pepper and hot sauce.

Cover with plastic wrap and set in the refrigerator overnight for the flavors to marry, or for a minimum of 6 hours. Adjust seasoning as needed before serving. Serve chilled.

BASIL GINGER ROASTED BUTTERNUT SQUASH WITH CRAB

"Best Soup/Best Seafood Soup" in 2012 at Souper Bowl XVIII

Prep Time: 1 hour
Cook Time: 40 minutes
Serves: 6–8

Ingredients:
1 cup olive oil
½ large yellow onion, diced small
1 tablespoon garlic, minced
2 tablespoons fresh ginger, peeled and minced
2 ribs celery, diced small
2 medium carrots, peeled and diced small
1 tablespoon ground ginger
1 tablespoon curry powder
½ tablespoon ground coriander
2 medium sweet potatoes, peeled and diced medium
1½ cups roasted butternut squash
6 cups vegetable stock
1 can coconut milk (13.5 ounces)
⅓ cup dry sherry wine
2 tablespoons rice wine vinegar
4 tablespoons fresh basil
Salt and pepper to taste
1 pound crab meat

Preheat oven to 350 degrees. Cut the butternut squash in half lengthwise and deseed. Coat the entire squash lightly with oil and place flesh side down onto a baking sheet. Roast for 30–45 minutes until flesh is soft. Let cool a bit then remove flesh from rind. Discard the rind. Place flesh in a small bowl and set aside.

In a large pot or Dutch oven heat the olive oil over medium–high heat until shimmering. Add onions, garlic, ginger, celery, and carrots, cooking 5 minutes until soft. Add the spices, cooking for 2 minutes until the spices start to stick to the pot. Add butternut squash and potatoes, stirring to mix well, around 2 minutes. Pour in the vegetable stock, coconut milk, and sherry wine, stirring well. Bring to a boil, reduce heat, and simmer for 20 minutes. Remove from heat and add rice wine vinegar and basil. Use an immersion blender to puree until smooth. You can also puree in a regular blender in batches and return to cooking pot. Add crabmeat and serve hot with a bit of fresh basil for garnish.

VEGETABLE AVOCADO AND CORN GAZPACHO

Active Prep Time: 1–1½ hours
Inactive Prep Time: 4–12 hours
Serves: 4–6

Ingredients:
2 zucchini, diced medium
3 yellow squash, seeds cored, diced medium
1 red or orange bell pepper, deseeded, diced medium
1 jalapeño, deseeded and minced
3 ears white corn, kernels removed from cobs
4 cups purified ice water
4 avocados
½ bunch fresh cilantro, chopped fine
Juice of 3 lemons
1 tablespoon ground coriander
1 tablespoon salt
1 teaspoon black pepper

Place 4 cups of water in the refrigerator to chill.

In a large bowl, combine zucchini, yellow squash, bell pepper, and jalapeño. Turn a small bowl upside down into the large bowl (it is okay if it covers some of the veggies). Hold the corn cob on the small bowl and use a knife to cut the kernels from the cob and into the veggie mixture. Set aside.

Cut the avocados in half. Remove the pit and spoon out the flesh into a medium-sized bowl. With a fork or potato masher, puree the avocados. Prep the cilantro and lemons and set aside.

Add a bit of ice water to the veggie mixture and with an immersion blender, pulse the veggies, but keep it somewhat chunky. Add the avocado puree, cilantro, lemon juice, all spices, and the rest of the ice water. Stir well. Cover and set in the refrigerator for 4 to 12 hours. Serve cold with a sprig of cilantro.

SPICED COCONUT CREAM GUAVA-LIME WITH CRISPY PLANTAINS

"Best Soup/Best Cream Soup" in 2013 at Souper Bowl XIX

Prep Time: 30 minutes
Cook Time: 45 minutes
Servings: 8–10

Ingredients:
¼ cup olive oil, halved
1 small yellow onion, diced fine
2 tablespoons fresh ginger, peeled and minced
½ small habañero pepper, deseeded and minced
2 tablespoons dried tarragon
2 tablespoon dried thyme
1 tablespoon ground coriander
½ tablespoon ground allspice
½ tablespoon cayenne
4 cups guava puree or nectar
3 cups vegetable stock
1 can coconut cream (13.5 ounces)
1 tablespoon kosher salt
1 teaspoon fresh lime juice

Heat 1/8 cup of olive oil in a soup pot over medium heat until shimmering. Add the onions, ginger and habañero pepper. Sauté with a wooden spoon until soft, about 3–5 minutes.

In a small bowl mix the spices together. Pour the reserved olive oil into the soup pot and add the spice mixture. Stir well, cooking 3–5 minutes until spices start to stick to the bottom of the pot. Pour in the guava puree and stir, loosening the spices. Add the vegetable stock and coconut cream, stirring well. Turn the heat up to medium-high and cook for 8–10 minutes. Add the salt, reduce heat to low, and simmer for 25 minutes. Remove from heat and stir in the lime juice.

For a better melding of flavors, cook this soup the day before, let cool, and refrigerate overnight. Use an immersion blender if you desire a smoother soup. Reheat and serve hot.

SMALL PLATES

These small plate recipes are based on the familiar street foods that you can buy from vendors all over East Africa. They are what we would call finger foods in America—small portions, easy to eat with your hands. They're almost a kind of snack and they've become very popular. Small plate foods are widely consumed to break the daily fast during Ramadan. In American restaurants, these fit into the appetizer category, although there's nothing like that in Lamu. This chapter contains several recipes straight from home.

PLANTAIN FRIED CRAB CAKES

Active Prep Time: 40 minutes
Inactive Prep Time: 10 minutes
Cook Time: 30 minutes
Serves: 6–8

It is helpful to have a pair of latex gloves on hand to mix this recipe.

Ingredients:
1 tablespoon olive oil
1 small red onion, finely diced
1 small jalapeño, finely diced
1 teaspoon garlic, minced
1 small ripe plantain, diced
¼ to ½ teaspoon cayenne pepper
½ cup cornstarch
2 whole eggs, beaten with a dash of milk
2 cups white corn meal
1 tablespoon dried parsley
1 tablespoon curry powder
½ teaspoon salt
Pinch black pepper
6 tablespoons mayonnaise
1 teaspoon salt
1 tub, typically 1 pound, of fresh lump crab meat
1 cup grape seed oil for frying

Heat the oil in a nonstick skillet over medium heat to shimmering. Add the onion, garlic, and jalapeño and sauté until soft, about 5 minutes. Add the plantain and cayenne and cook for another 3 minutes. Remove from heat, pour into a large bowl, and let cool 5–10 minutes.

Meanwhile, set up three bowls containing:
1: ½ cup cornstarch
2: 2 eggs, beaten with a dash of milk
3: 2 cups cornmeal with the parsley, curry, salt, and pepper mixed in
Don your latex gloves. Add the mayonnaise, salt, and crab meat to the cooling onion mixture and mix well by hand.

Form the crab mixture into patties about the size of the palm of your hand. Dredge each patty in the cornstarch, the egg, and then the cornmeal mixture. Set aside on a plate.

In a skillet over medium-high heat, bring the oil temperature to between 325–350 degrees. Fry the crab patties in batches until they are golden and crispy and rise to the top of the oil. Drain on paper towels.

Serve hot. Consider serving with a sauce or chutney from Chapter 7.

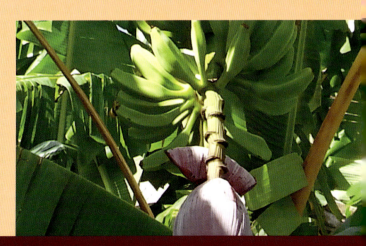

JAMBO CAFE 57

SWAHILI BAJIA

Bajia, pronounced "ba–jee–a," is an African street food like falafel.

Active Prep Time: 20 minutes
Inactive Prep Time: 8–12 hours
Cook Time: 20–25 minutes
Serves: 6–8

Ingredients:
1 cup black-eyed peas, dried
2 cups water
½ or 1 whole small red onion, chopped fine
1 jalapeño, deseeded and chopped fine
½ tablespoon fresh garlic, minced
1 tablespoon ground coriander
½ tablespoon curry powder
¼ cup fresh cilantro, chopped
Water as needed
2 cups grape seed or other high heat oil for frying
Salt to taste

Soak the black-eyed peas overnight in water. Remove any husks and peas that rise to the top. In the morning, drain the peas and replace the water. The peas can soak until active prep time.

Drain the peas and place in a blender with the onion, garlic, and jalapeño. Add water as necessary to blend until smooth. The batter should be thick enough to form into balls or patties, not watery.

Transfer into a bowl and add the coriander, curry, cilantro and a dash of salt. Mix together by hand and set aside. The traditional mixing method is to use your hands. Give it a try!

In a deep pan for frying heat the oil on medium-high heat to 375 degrees. Use a tablespoon or small cookie scoop to place the batter in the hot oil, making balls, which will go straight to the bottom of the pan. When the balls rise use tongs to turn them over. Cook the Bajia to a golden brown on all sides. Remove from oil and drain on paper towels.

Serve hot with Green Mango Coconut Chutney, see page 71.

SPICED BATTERED POTATOES

Prep Time: 20–25 minutes
Cook Time: 10–15 minutes
Serves: 4

Ingredients:
2 large russet potatoes, peeled
1 teaspoon curry powder
½ teaspoon ground cayenne
½ teaspoon ground turmeric
1 tablespoon fresh minced garlic
1 teaspoon salt
½ cup flour
¾ cups water
Grape seed or other high heat oil for frying

In a medium-sized saucepan bring some salted water to a boil. Peel the potatoes and cut into quarters. Place the potatoes in boiling water and bring back to a boil. Parboil the potatoes for 8–10 minutes. Drain and let cool for 2–3 minutes, then cut the quartered potatoes into ½ inch chunks.

In a medium-sized mixing bowl combine all dry ingredients and set aside. Heat a deep-bottomed cast iron skillet on medium heat and add the cooking oil, heating to 375 degrees.

Pour the water into the bowl of dry ingredients and mix well with a spoon to form a batter. Dip the potatoes into the batter and, in two batches, deep fry to a golden brown, about 5 minutes per batch. Drain on paper towels. Add salt to taste.

Serve as a starter or for breakfast, with eggs.

CURRIED GOAT CHEESE CAKES

Prep Time: 15 minutes
Cook Time: 10–15 minutes
Serves: 4

Ingredients:
- 1 10½-ounce log of chevre (goat cheese)
- ¾ cup panko bread crumbs
- ¼ cup salted pistachios
- 1 tablespoon curry powder
- 1 tablespoon dried parsley
- 1 teaspoon salt (add only if you cannot find unsalted pistachios)
- ¼ cup flour
- 1 egg
- Grape seed oil for frying
- 2 cups salad greens of your choice, separated into fourths
- Balsamic vinegar to taste

In a food processor, blend the panko, pistachios, and spices. Set aside in a medium-sized bowl. Place the flour in another medium-sized bowl. Crack the egg into another bowl and beat well.

Remove the goat cheese from the refrigerator and slice open the package on all sides so the cheese retains its log shape. With a sharp knife, slice the goat cheese into ½ to ¾ inch rounds or evenly into 8 rounds.

Dredge the rounds by dipping each round first into the flour, coating both sides. Dip in the egg wash, coating both sides. Finally, coat both sides with the panko-pistachio mixture. Set on a plate and repeat the process with all remaining chevre rounds.

Heat a deep-bottomed frying pan over medium heat and add approximately 2 inches of vegetable oil. When the oil reaches a temperature of 375 degrees, fry the rounds in two batches of four. Place the rounds in the oil so they are not touching and fry for 1 minute. Flip and fry for an additional 1 minute. Remove and drain on paper towels. Repeat the process with the next four rounds.

Place the salad greens on 4 plates and drizzle with a well-aged balsamic vinegar. Place two chevre rounds on top of the greens.

CINNAMON DUSTED PLANTAINS

Prep Time: 30 minutes
Cook Time: 20–30 minutes
Serves: 4–6

Ingredients:
4 medium to large plantains, yellow with brown spots, firm to the touch but not hard
2 tablespoons cinnamon
1 tablespoon sugar
Butter or grape seed oil

Combine the cinnamon and sugar in a small bowl and set aside. Prepare the plantains by cutting off both ends and removing the skin. Slice lengthwise into strips about ¼-inch wide, following the curve of the plantain. You can also cut the plantain in half and slice lengthwise.

Plantains can be fried in butter or deep fried in oil at a temperature ranging from 365 to 375 degrees. Cook the strips in batches and let them soften all the way through for 2–8 minutes, depending on your cooking method.

Dust with cinnamon and sugar mixture. Serve hot.

CASSAVA FRIES

Prep Time: 15–20 minutes
Cook Time: 30–45 minutes
Serves: 4–6

Ingredients:
2 medium cassava (yuca, manioc)
Grape seed or other high heat oil for frying
Cayenne pepper to taste
Salt to taste
1 lemon, cut into wedges

Use a sharp knife to cut both ends off the cassava. Cut each root in half or thirds. Tap into the skin with a knife and then peel the skin in a round or cut the skin off in sheets, rotating the cassava root. Once peeled, cut the root lengthwise in half and then again. Remove the hard core. Cut the root into pieces, "steak fries" style.

Over medium heat use a deep-bottomed cast iron skillet or frying pan to heat the oil to 375 degrees. Fry the cassava in batches until golden brown and tender inside, 13–15 minutes for each batch. Drain on paper towels.

Sprinkle or toss the cassava fries with a mixture of cayenne and salt and then sprinkle with lemon juice. Serve hot.

Alternative Toppings: Try cumin, curry, garam masala or any spice mixture that suits your fancy.

PEELING CASSAVA ROOT

1. Use a sharp knife!

2. Slice Cassava into manageable pieces for your hands.

3. Slice into a side, not too deep, then turn the knife and work around the root.

4. The bark of the root will peel off like paper off a birch tree.

5. Alternatively, slice off the bark on all sides.

6. Cut the peeled cassava in half and remove the central core.

MARINATED GARLIC AND BASIL GRILLED SHRIMP

Active Prep Time: 25–30 minutes
Inactive Prep Time: 2 hours
Cook Time: 5 minutes
Serves: 4

Ingredients:
1 pound shrimp, peeled and deveined (16–20 shrimp in a pound)
1 tablespoon fresh garlic, chopped
1 cup fresh sweet basil, chopped
1 teaspoon freshly cracked black pepper
1 teaspoon salt
½ cup olive oil
Bamboo skewers

Peel and devein the shrimp and set aside in a bowl. Mix all other ingredients and pour over the shrimp. Cover and marinate for 2 hours in refrigerator.

Soak the skewers in a pan of water 15 minutes prior to cooking.

Remove the shrimp from the marinade and place on skewers. Cook the shrimp on your grill for 2–4 minutes per side. You can also toss the shrimp in a skillet for 2–4 minutes over medium heat.

Serve with a garnish of fresh basil.

PEANUT CHICKEN KEBABS

Active Prep Time: 30 minutes
Inactive Prep Time: 2 hours
Cook Time: 20 minutes
Serves: 4

Ingredients:
1 pound chicken
4 cups water
2 teaspoons salt
2 tablespoons sugar
1 tablespoon ground ginger
½ teaspoon ground allspice
1 teaspoon dried thyme
1 tablespoon ground coriander
½ teaspoon cayenne
1 tablespoon sweet paprika
¾ cups roasted and salted peanuts
½ teaspoon freshly cracked black pepper
1 teaspoon salt (to taste if using salted nuts)
3 tablespoons fresh cilantro, chopped
Juice from ½ fresh lemon
1 teaspoon honey
2 tablespoons olive oil
Bamboo skewers

In this recipe, we use a cooking technique called *brining* to tenderize the chicken. In a large bowl or container, mix water, salt, and sugar stirring well. Add the chicken and brine for 2 hours. Remove the chicken from the brine, cut into thin slices, and set aside in a bowl.

Place the skewers in a pan of water 15 minutes before cook time. In a blender, blend all dry ingredients and add the fresh cilantro, lemon juice, honey, and oil. Toss the chicken with the spice mixture. Note that the spice mixture will be chunky. Place chicken strips on skewers.

You can use a stove-top grill pan or your outside grill. The cooking time will be the same. Heat the grill pan or your grill and cook the skewers for 5 minutes per side until the chicken is firm.

7

CHUTNEYS AND SAUCES

Fruit was always available where I grew up, even when other foods were too expensive or hard to find. In developing chutneys and sauces, here I went back to my roots, and I use fruit rather than sugar or honey as the sweeteners. Mango, coconut, pineapple—they all combine very well with spices to give the chutneys and sauces a sweet but citrusy, tangy, unusual flavor and texture. Fruits are plentiful in the Caribbean islands, too, and there are definite Caribbean notes in these recipes.

GREEN MANGO COCONUT CHUTNEY

Active Prep Time: 20–30 minutes
Inactive Prep Time: 1 hour
Serves: 4–6

Ingredients:
2 unripe mangoes
1 large brown coconut
1 serrano or jalapeño chile, deseeded and minced
½ cup fresh cilantro, chopped
Juice of 1–2 lemons to taste, strained
Salt to taste

Peel the mangoes with a paring knife. Cut the mangoes into small pieces and set aside in a large bowl. Discard the pits.

Crack open the coconut and follow the directions on the following page "How to Open a Coconut." *Remember!* Do not use a paring or sharp kitchen knife or you could injure yourself.

Once the coconut flesh is removed from the hull, peel any remaining brown skin off with a vegetable peeler. Cut any large white chunks into smaller pieces.

Place the mango, coconut and all other ingredients in a blender and pulse until slightly chunky or smooth. Place in a bowl, cover, and chill for at least 1 hour.

Serve as a topping for Swahili Bajia, (see page 59) or grilled fish or chicken.

How to Choose a Coconut
1. A fresh and ready coconut should feel heavy for its size. Put the coconut up to your ear and shake; you should hear a sloshing sound. A good coconut has a lot of juice inside, at least a cup. If you don't hear anything select another coconut.
2. Look at the 3 eyes on one end of the coconut. One of the eyes is called the 'soft eye;' it is the one that doesn't have the shell slightly raised around it. The 'soft eye' should look clean without any discoloration.
3. The shell of the coconut should look brown with no overtones of gray or other discoloration. If your coconut has a white shell, then you've simply chosen a white coconut, but all other selection criteria apply. Ensure that the coconut doesn't have any cracks or stains on it where there might have been a fracture.

HOW TO OPEN A COCONUT

1. Setup a bowl to catch the juice, a stick with which to strike, and the coconut.

2. Strike the coconut with the stick (you can also use a hammer) over the bowl.

3. Once the coconut cracks, continue to strike until you can separate the ha[lves]

4. Separate the halves and pour any remaining juice into the bowl.

5. The coconut insides should be a pure and vibrant white.

6. Use a butter knife to separate the coco[nut] flesh from the hull.

FRESH MANGO AND GINGER CHUTNEY

Prep Time: 20 minutes
Cook Time: 10 minutes
Serves: 4–6

Ingredients:
2 large ripe mangoes
½ cup fresh ginger, grated
½ red bell pepper, deseeded and diced small
½ small to medium red onion, diced small
1 serrano pepper, deseeded and chopped fine
½ cup rice wine vinegar
½ cup water
½ teaspoon cayenne pepper
3 cinnamon sticks
¼ cup sugar
½ cup fresh cilantro, chopped
Zest of one lime
Juice of one lime
Salt and pepper to taste

Peel the mangoes and cut into small cubes, discarding the pits. Set aside in a large bowl.

Place ginger, bell pepper, onion, Serrano pepper, vinegar, water, cayenne, cinnamon and sugar in a medium sauce pan. Bring to a boil, reduce heat, and cook for 5 minutes until all ingredients soften. With a wooden spoon, mix in the mango, cilantro, salt, and pepper. If the mixture is too dry, add a bit more water. Cook on low for an additional 5 minutes, stirring constantly. Remove from heat, add lime zest, lime juice, and salt and pepper to taste.

Serve hot or cold.

How to Choose a Mango
1. Disregard the green and red colors; it is not the best indicator of ripeness.
2. Squeeze the mango gently; a ripe mango will give slightly.
3. The feel will be similar to ripening peaches or avocados.
4. Ripe mangoes can have a fruity aroma at their stem ends.

CILANTRO MANGO LIME SAUCE

Active Prep Time: 20 minutes
Inactive Prep Time: 2 hours
Serves: 4–6

Ingredients:
2 very ripe mangoes, peeled, pitted, and sliced
1 bunch cilantro, large stems removed
3 cloves garlic, quartered
2 jalapeño, deseeded and halved
Juice of one lime
2 tablespoons light olive oil
Salt and black pepper to taste

In a large bowl mix everything together and use an immersion blender to blend until smooth. Or place all ingredients in a regular blender and blend until smooth. Add lime to taste.

Serve as a sauce over fish, chicken or vegetables, or as a dip for chips or *bajia*.

PINEAPPLE COCONUT RUM CHUTNEY

Prep Time: 20 minutes
Cook Time: 20 minutes
Serves: 4–6

Ingredients:
1 fresh pineapple, peeled, cored, and diced small
½ medium red onion, diced small
½ teaspoon cayenne pepper
½ cup sweetened coconut flakes
¼ cup brown sugar
1 tablespoon fresh ginger, chopped fine
1 tablespoon dried tarragon
½ cup rice wine vinegar
½ cup water or pineapple juice
½ cup Jamaican spiced rum (according to taste)

In a medium saucepan combine all ingredients and bring to a boil. Reduce heat and simmer for 15 minutes, stirring every few minutes.

Serve hot or cold over fish, chicken, or with chips.

How to Pick the Perfect Pineapple
1. External color does not indicate ripeness
2. Choose a fresh-looking pineapple with green leaves and a firm shell
3. Yes, the freshest-looking pineapple could be green in color
4. If storing at room temperature, use within a few days
5. If refrigerating, use within 6 days

GRILLED TOMATILLO SPICED MANGO SAUCE

Prep Time: 1½ hours
Cook Time: 10–15 minutes
Serves: 4–6

Ingredients:
8 fresh tomatillos
1 tablespoon olive oil
Dash of salt and freshly cracked black pepper
2 fresh mangoes, peeled, pitted, and chopped
½ tablespoon fresh garlic, chopped
½ fresh habañero chili, halved, and deseeded
½ branch fresh cilantro
3 green onion fronds
2 tablespoons fresh lemon juice
Salt and pepper to taste

Bring 3 cups of water to a boil in a medium to large saucepan. Peel the papery skin from the tomatillos and discard. Drop the tomatillos into the boiling water for 1–3 minutes. Scoop out with a slotted spoon and drain.

As a well-seasoned cast iron skillet heats over medium-high heat, slice the tomatillos in half and mix them with olive oil, salt, and pepper in a bowl. Cook the tomatillos, 1–2 minutes per side, remove from pan, and set aside.

Peel, pit, and chop the mangoes. Place mangoes and tomatillos in a blender with all remaining ingredients and puree. Place in a bowl, cover with plastic wrap, and let the flavors meld for about an hour.

The sauce can be served chilled or at room temperature.

This salsa is fantastic on grilled fish such as snapper or mahi mahi, or as a garnish for fish tacos or with chips.

How to Choose a Tomatillo
Choose smaller tomatillos, they're sweeter. The flesh of the tomatillo beneath its husk should be firm and bright green. The husk should feel tacky to the touch. Discard a tomatillo with a yellow or dry-looking husk.
Discard a tomatillo whose flesh appears to be withered or dried out.
Discard a tomatillo that does not fit firmly in its husks.

SIDES

Side dishes do not exist in many cultures, at least not the way we think of them in America. Actually, the starchy foods that we call side dishes here are often main dishes in poorer cultures, where protein is expensive and a rare luxury, as it was for my family when I was a child. My mother cooked heaping platters of foods like *fufu*, rice, *ugali* and *roti*, made delicious and tempting because they were accompanied by deeply spiced sauces. In America, sides accompany main dishes, usually a protein like fish, meat, or chicken. These sides were developed to complement the highly spiced and savory stews, sauces, and main dishes we regularly serve at Jambo Café.

GINGER RUM SWEET POTATOES

Prep Time: 15 minutes
Cook Time: 45 minutes
Serves: 4–6

Ingredients:
4 medium sweet potatoes, washed and rubbed with oil
2 tablespoons butter
½ teaspoon salt
1 tablespoon ground ginger
½ teaspoon ground allspice
½ cup coconut cream or heavy cream (optional)
¼ cup Jamaican spiced rum

Preheat oven to 350 degrees. On a small sheet pan, roast sweet potatoes for about 35–45 minutes until soft. Remove from oven and open the potatoes to cool slightly. Remove flesh from skins and place in a bowl. Add all other ingredients and mash by hand or put in a food processor for extra creamy potatoes. Serve hot.

CURRIED MASHED RED POTATOES

Prep Time: 20 minutes
Cook Time: 20 minutes
Serves: 4–6

Ingredients:
8–10 medium red potatoes with their skins, cut into quarters
2 tablespoons curry powder
2 tablespoons butter, melted
1 tablespoon salt
½ cup coconut cream or heavy cream
2 tablespoons fresh chopped chives

In a large-sized saucepan, bring salted water (enough to cover the potatoes) to boil and cook the potatoes until soft, about 15–20 minutes. Leave the skins on and smash with a potato masher.

Melt the butter and add the curry and salt, stirring well. Add the butter mixture, the cream or coconut milk, and mix well. Garnish with the chives. Serve hot.

SAUTÉED SPINACH WITH GARLIC

Prep Time: 10 minutes
Cook Time: Up to 10 minutes
Serves: 4–6

Ingredients:
2 tablespoons olive oil
1 teaspoon garlic, minced
2 pounds fresh spinach, cleaned and trimmed
½ teaspoon freshly cracked black pepper

Heat a medium to large skillet over medium heat, add the oil and heat until shimmering. Add the garlic and cook for 10–15 seconds. Add the spinach, salt, and pepper. Toss and coat. Let the spinach cook down until tender, about 5 minutes.

BALSAMIC GARLIC MARINATED GRILLED ASPARAGUS

Active Prep Time: 5–10 minutes
Inactive Prep Time: 2 hours
Cook Time: 5–8 minutes
Serves: 4–6

Ingredients:
1 pound asparagus
½ tablespoon fresh minced garlic
¼ cup quality balsamic vinegar
1 teaspoon black pepper
Salt to taste
Fresh parsley for garnish

Remove ½ to 1 inch of the stems from the base of the asparagus, including any part that is woody, by gently bending the end of each spear until it snaps naturally.

Cover the bottom of a large frying pan with an inch of water and bring to a boil. Place asparagus in the pan and cook for 2–5 minutes or until bright green. Add cold water to the pan to stop the cooking process.

Drain in a colander. Rinse asparagus with cold water, let drain. Place asparagus in a flat glass dish. Mix all other ingredients and pour over the asparagus. Cover and place in the refrigerator to chill and marinate for 2 hours.

Serve cold or toss the mixture in a pan for a couple of minutes to reheat.

LAMU STYLE COCONUT SPINACH

Prep Time: 15 minutes
Cook Time: 15 minutes
Serves: 4–6

Ingredients:
2 pounds spinach, cleaned and trimmed
2 Roma tomatoes, diced
1 teaspoon garlic, minced
1 teaspoon curry powder
¼ teaspoon salt
1 cup coconut cream

Place the spinach, tomatoes, garlic, curry powder and salt in a large skillet over medium heat. Cover and steam for 3–5 minutes.

Uncover and cook for 2–3 minutes to let water evaporate. Turn heat to low, add the coconut cream, and stir well. Cook on low for an additional 3 minutes. Serve hot.

COCONUT GOAT CHEESE CORN MEAL

Prep Time: 10 minutes
Cook Time: 10 minutes
Serves: 4–6

Ingredients:
4 cups water
1 teaspoon salt
1 teaspoon freshly cracked black pepper
1 tablespoon butter
1½ cups white corn meal
1 cup coconut milk
½ cup goat cheese (chevre)
Fresh parsley for garnish

In a medium-sized saucepan bring the water to a boil. Add salt, pepper, and butter. Once the butter melts, turn the heat to low and add the corn meal, stirring until softened. Pour in the coconut milk, stirring constantly. Add the goat cheese and mix well. Remove from heat. The corn meal mixture should be soft. Garnish with parsley.

COCONUT BASMATI RICE

Prep Time: 10 minutes
Cook Time: 30 minutes
Serves: 4–6

Ingredients:
1 cup white basmati rice
1 teaspoon olive oil
2 cups water
1½ cups coconut milk
1 teaspoon salt

Heat the olive oil over medium heat in a medium-sized saucepan until shimmering. Add the dry rice and stir constantly until the rice turns a bit whiter. Add the water, coconut milk, and salt. Bring to a boil, then turn to low and simmer covered for 15–20 minutes or until liquid has evaporated.

STEWS

Some of Jambo Café's most popular dishes are stews, even though there is no food category called stews in Africa. The chicken curry and lamb and goat stews are always best-sellers in the restaurant. In fact, our goat stew was featured on The Food Channel's *Diners, Drive-Ins and Dives.* I developed my stews from sauces my mother cooked; it was a natural progression. They simmered in a big pot that included everything that was available for the meal, most often beans or lentils, or small amounts of fish or beef, always served to make the breads especially delicious. No matter which part of Africa they may be from, Africans visiting Jambo are thrilled by the stews we serve, which remind them of home and are the ultimate comfort food.

JAMBO COCONUT CHICKEN CURRY

Prep Time: 1 hour
Cook Time: 45 minutes
Serves: 4–6

Ingredients:
3 pounds boneless chicken thighs and breasts cut into 1½ inch cubes
½ cup olive oil
½ large yellow onion, diced small
1 tablespoon minced garlic
2 tablespoons curry
¼ teaspoon cayenne pepper
1 tablespoon ground coriander
1 tablespoon ground cumin
1 tablespoon ginger powder
2 tablespoons tomato paste
1 cup Roma tomatoes, diced fine
1 tablespoon kosher salt
1 can coconut milk (13.5 ounces)
1 cup chicken or vegetable stock
Olive oil for cooking

Heat olive oil in a deep-bottomed skillet or Dutch oven over medium heat until shimmering. Sauté the onion and garlic 3–5 minutes until soft. Add the spices from the curry to the ginger powder, mixing well and cooking 3–5 minutes until spices start to stick to the pot. Stir in the tomato paste until softened, 2–3 minutes. Reduce heat if needed. Add the tomato, cooking 5–7 minutes, stirring occasionally.

Stir in coconut milk, and the chicken or vegetable stock, mixing thoroughly. Turn up heat to medium-high and boil for 5–10 minutes, stirring occasionally. Reduce heat and add the salt, simmering for 20 minutes, stirring occasionally.

While the sauce is simmering, sprinkle the chicken with curry powder, turmeric, and salt. In a large frying pan, heat some olive oil until shimmering. Cook the chicken in batches until the flesh is firm. Remove from pan and drain on paper towels. Transfer chicken to the curry sauce and serve.

For best results, cover and place in the refrigerator so the flavors can marry. Reheat over a low-medium heat.

Serve hot with basmati rice and Sautéed Spinach with Garlic (see page 81) or Balsamic Garlic Marinated Grilled Asparagus (see page 82).

RAS EL HANOUT CHICKEN AND OLIVE STEW

Inactive Prep Time: 2 to 24 hours
Active Prep Time: 45 minutes
Cook Time: 1 hour
Serves: 4–6

Ingredients for the Ras el Hanout marinade:
2 pounds chicken breast
1½ tablespoons of Ras El Hanout spice blend, see page 35
3 tablespoons olive oil

Cut the chicken into 1-inch chunks and place in a medium-sized bowl. Mix the spice mixture with the oil and pour over the chicken. Toss by hand to ensure that the spices and chicken mix well. Cover and place in the refrigerator for a minimum of 2 hours and up to 24 hours.

Ingredients for the stew:
½ cup unsalted butter
1 large red or yellow onion, diced large
1 teaspoon fresh garlic, minced
1½ tablespoons fresh ginger, minced
1 whole red bell pepper, deseeded and diced large
1½ tablespoons of Ras El Hanout spice blend
2 tablespoons tomato paste
2 medium-sized sweet potatoes, peeled and cut into 1-inch cubes
½ cup apricots, quartered
½ cup raisins
3–4 cups chicken stock
2 tablespoons arrowroot powder
½ pound mixed green olives, pitted (Any olives will do. Use what you like. Cut the olives in half or quarters if they're exceptionally large.)

In a soup pot or large Dutch oven melt the butter over medium heat. Add onion, garlic, ginger, and bell pepper, and cook until soft, about 3–5 minutes. Add Ras el Hanout spice blend and cook 2 minutes. Stir in tomato paste until mixed well. Add sweet potatoes and cook for 5–7 minutes. Stir in apricots and raisins and cook for 2 minutes. Pour in 3 cups of chicken stock, mixing well, and cook for 3–5 minutes to heat stock until just before boiling. Pull a cup of the warm stock into a cup or liquid measuring cup and mix in arrowroot powder until dissolved. Pour back into stew pot, stirring well. Bring to a boil and cook 5 minutes on high heat, turn heat to low, and simmer for 30–40 minutes, stirring occasionally. Add more stock if stew is becoming too thick.

While the stew is simmering, heat a large frying pan over medium heat and add a bit of olive oil. Cook the chicken pieces in batches until firm. Drain on paper towels. Add the chicken and the olives to the stew and simmer for an additional 10 minutes. Turn the stew off and let sit for 10 minutes to allow the flavors to marry.

If you let the stew sit in the refrigerator overnight it will be even more robust the next day. Add salt to taste.

SPICE COCONUT PEANUT CHICKEN STEW

"Best Soup/Best Savory Soup" in 2010 at Souper Bowl XVI

Prep Time: 1 hour
Inactive Prep Time: 2–8 hours
Cook Time: 45 minutes
Serves: 4–6

Ingredients:
3 pounds chicken thighs and breasts, trimmed and cut into 1½ inch cubes
½ large yellow onion, diced small
1 tablespoon minced garlic
½ cup blended olive oil
½ tablespoon cayenne pepper
1 tablespoon ground coriander
1 tablespoon ground cumin
½ tablespoon ground allspice
1 teaspoon dried thyme
1 tablespoon sweet paprika
2 tablespoons fresh ginger, diced fine
2 tablespoons tomato paste
1 cup Roma tomatoes, diced fine
2 cups peanut butter
1 tablespoon kosher salt
1 can coconut milk (13.5 ounces)
1 cup chicken or vegetable stock
Olive oil for cooking

Heat a large skillet on medium heat to heat the olive oil until shimmering. Sauté the onion and garlic 3–5 minutes until soft. Stir in the spices from the cayenne to the paprika. Add the ginger and mix well. If the spice mixture seems extra dry, add a bit more oil.

Cook for 3–5 minutes until spices begin to stick to the pot. Add the tomato paste and stir until softened, 2–3 minutes. Reduce heat if needed. Stir in the tomato and peanut butter, mixing thoroughly and cook for 5–7 minutes. Stir occasionally.

Pour in the coconut milk, chicken or vegetable stock and stir well. Turn up heat to medium-high and boil for 5–10 minutes, stirring occasionally. Reduce heat, add the salt, and simmer for 20 minutes, stirring occasionally.

While the sauce is simmering, season the chicken with salt and pepper. In a large skillet heat the olive oil until shimmering. In batches, cook the chicken until the flesh is firm. Remove from pan and drain on paper towels. Transfer the chicken into the coconut peanut sauce, mixing well.

Cover and place in the refrigerator for 2 to 8 hours for the flavors to marry. Reheat over a low-medium heat and serve hot with basmati rice and Sautéed Spinach with Garlic (see page 81).

MOROCCAN LAMB STEW

Active Prep Time: 30 minutes–1 hour
Inactive Prep Time: 2–12 hours
Cook Time: 1¾ hours
Serves: 4–6

Ingredients for the marinade:
¼ cup oil
4 pounds leg of lamb, cut into cubes, or lamb stew meat
2 tablespoons curry
1 tablespoon cinnamon
1 tablespoon ground cumin
1 tablespoon ground coriander
1 teaspoon ground allspice
1 teaspoon ground thyme
½ teaspoon cayenne

If using a leg of lamb, debone, remove the fat back and the silverskin, and cut into 1½-inch cubes.

Blend all spices together in a small bowl. Mix with ½ cup olive oil to make a paste. Place lamb cubes in a medium bowl with the spice mixture, cover with plastic wrap, and marinate for 2 hours to overnight in the refrigerator.

Optional: If desired, use the lamb bone to make a lamb stock to replace the beef stock in the stew. In a soup pot pour 6 cups of cold water, the lamb bone, 3 ribs of celery, 3 carrots, quartered, 1 onion, quartered, ½ to 1 tablespoon of salt, 10–15 peppercorns, and a cinnamon stick. Bring to a boil and simmer for a couple of hours. If making the stew the next day, remove from heat, cover, and refrigerate.

Ingredients for the stew:
¼ cup olive oil
1 small yellow onion, diced fine
1 tablespoon garlic, diced fine
½ cup tomato paste
3–4 cups chicken stock
3–4 cups beef or lamb stock
1 medium sweet potato, peeled and diced
2 cups cooked garbanzo beans
½ cup dried apricots
½ cup dried raisins

Remove the lamb marinade mixture from the refrigerator. Over medium heat in a stew pot heat the oil until shimmering then add the onions and garlic, cooking until soft, 3–5 minutes. Stir in the lamb and separate the chunks with a wooden spoon. Brown the meat, allowing spices to release, about 5–7 minutes.

(continued on next page)

Stir in the tomato paste, scraping the spices from the bottom of the pot, cooking an additional 3 minutes. Begin with 3 cups each of the beef/lamb and chicken stock, bring to a boil, then reduce heat to low and cook for 1 hour. As the stew thickens, add more stock if it starts to become too dry.

Add the sweet potatoes and garbanzo beans and simmer for 20 minutes. Add apricots and raisins and simmer for an additional 10 minutes.

Serve hot over rice or *ugali*. For best results, cover and refrigerate overnight to allow the flavors to marry.

BISON MEATBALLS IN MOROCCAN SPICE STEW

This recipe was created by Chef Obo for Thunder Chef 2014, a benefit for the Pojoaque Pueblo Youth Hoop Dancers.

Prep Time: 1 hour
Cook Time: 1½ hours
Serves: 8–10

Ingredients for the meatballs:
2 tablespoons blended olive oil
1 medium to large red onion, diced small
1 jalapeño, deseeded and diced small
1 tablespoon fresh garlic, minced
1 tablespoon pili pili spice mix (see page 36)
1 tablespoon ground cinnamon
3 tablespoons fennel seeds, toasted
¾ cup panko breadcrumbs
2 pounds ground bison
2 eggs
1 tablespoon tomato paste
1 tablespoon salt

Preheat the oven to 350 degrees. In a large sauté pan add oil, onion, garlic, and jalapeño and cook until soft. Add the pili pili, cinnamon, fennel, and panko and mix well. Remove from heat.

In a large bowl, mix the ground bison with the eggs, tomato paste, and salt. Stir in the onion and spice mixture. Form into meatballs about 1-inch in diameter and place in a baking dish coated with a bit of olive oil. Bake for 12–15 minutes.

Ingredients for the stew:
½ cup blended olive oil
1 medium yellow onion, diced
1 tablespoon garlic, minced
1½ teaspoons ground coriander
½ teaspoon dried thyme
1 teaspoon ground ginger
1 teaspoon ground allspice
½ teaspoon cayenne
2 tablespoons tomato paste
2 cups Roma tomatoes, diced
2 medium sweet potatoes, peeled and diced large
1 cup chicken stock
2 cups beef stock
2 bay leaves
1–2 tablespoons arrowroot powder
Salt and pepper to taste

In a soup pot or large Dutch oven heat the olive oil until shimmering. Add the onion and garlic and cook for 3–5 minutes until soft. Mix in all the spices (excluding

(continued on next page)

the bay leaves) and cook for another 2–3 minutes. Add the tomato paste, mixing well. Add the tomatoes, cooking for 3–5 minutes, stirring occasionally until softened. Mix in the sweet potato and cook for 5–7 minutes. Pour in both the chicken and beef stock, add the bay leaves, bring to a boil, and reduce heat to low. Cover and simmer for 30 minutes.

Ladle a cup of stock from the soup pot into liquid measuring cup. Begin with 1 tablespoon of arrowroot powder and stir well until all of the powder is dissolved. Pour the mixture back into the stock. It should immediately begin to slightly thicken. If you want the stew thicker, do another round of arrowroot powder.

Add the bison meatballs. Cover and reduce heat to low and simmer for an additional 10–15 minutes. Add salt and pepper to taste.

Serve hot with coconut basmati rice, *ugali*, *fufu* or mashed potatoes

SLOW COOKED BEEF IN AFRICAN SPICE BLEND

Active Prep Time: 30 minutes
Inactive Prep Time: 2–24 hours
Cook Time: 3½ hours
Serves: 4–6

Ingredients for the marinade:
2 pounds top sirloin or rump roast
2 tablespoons sweet smoked paprika
1 tablespoon coriander
1 tablespoon cumin
1 tablespoon curry powder
½ tablespoon cinnamon
½ tablespoon ginger
1 teaspoon dried thyme
¾ teaspoon cayenne
½ teaspoon dried rosemary
1 tablespoon salt
½ teaspoon black pepper
2 tablespoons garlic, minced
Olive oil

Trim the excess fat from the sirloin and cut into 2-inch cubes. Place in a large bowl and set aside. In a small bowl mix together all the spices plus the garlic. Dry rub the spice mixture into the meat, adding enough olive oil to moisten the chunks of meat. Cover and refrigerate from 2–24 hours.

Ingredients to slow-cook the beef:
¼ cup olive oil
1 yellow onion, chopped medium
3 cloves garlic, minced
3 tablespoons tomato paste
2 cups beef stock
1 cup red wine (South African blend would be best)

Preheat the oven to 275 degrees. In a deep cast iron skillet or Dutch oven heat the oil over medium-high heat until shimmering. Add the onions and garlic and sauté until soft, about 3–5 minutes. Add the beef cubes and cook until all sides are browned. Add the tomato paste, stirring well until softened; then pour in the beef stock and red wine. Bring to boil, reduce heat, and simmer 5 minutes. Cover and put in the oven and slow-cook for 3 hours.

Serve hot over basmati rice or with another starch of your choice.

ETHIOPIAN SPICED SEAFOOD GUMBO

(Gluten Free)

Prep Time: 20–25 minutes
Cook Time: 40–45 minutes
Serves: 6–8

Ingredients:
½ pound butter
1 cup rice flour or rice flour blend
½ cup olive oil
1 yellow onion, diced small
1 tablespoon fresh garlic, minced
2 red bell peppers, deseeded and diced small
4 ribs celery, diced small
2 tablespoons ground cumin
1 tablespoon ground coriander
1 tablespoon dried thyme
1½ tablespoons dried oregano
½ tablespoon red chili powder
½ teaspoon freshly cracked ground pepper
3 cups Roma tomatoes, diced
2 cups fresh okra, sliced
6 cups vegetable stock
½ tablespoon salt, additional to taste
1 pound baby shrimp
1 pound white fish
½–1 pound lump crab meat
¼ cup fresh lemon juice

Melt the butter in a large Dutch oven or soup pot over medium-high heat. Make a roux by whisking or stirring the butter with a wooden spoon, while adding the flour; the mixture should foam up. Turn the heat down to medium, stirring or whisking constantly. The mixture will turn golden and then to a light brown. Be careful not to scorch the mixture; turn down the heat if needed. Cook for 15 minutes to a light brown roux. If you prefer a darker roux then continue cooking until desired shade is reached.

Pour in the olive oil and add the onion, garlic, peppers, and celery, cooking until soft, about 5 minutes. Add the spices, mixing well and cooking for an additional 2 minutes. Add the tomatoes and cook 5 minutes to soften. Stir in the okra, pour in the vegetable stock, and add the salt. Bring to a boil, then reduce heat and simmer 13–15 minutes. Turn off heat and stir in the shrimp, white fish, and crab meat, and let sit for 5 minutes. Stir in the lemon juice. Serve hot.

CURRIED LENTILS

Prep Time: 1 hour
Cook Time: 1½ hours
Serves: 6–8

Ingredients:
2 cups dried green lentils
8 cups water
1 tablespoon salt
1 tablespoon ground cumin
1 tablespoon ground turmeric
2½ tablespoons ground coriander
2½ tablespoons curry powder
½ tablespoon ginger powder
½ teaspoon salt
½ cup olive oil
1 large yellow onion, diced small
1 tablespoon garlic, minced
4 ribs celery, diced small
2 medium carrots, diced small
3 tablespoons tomato paste
1½ cans coconut milk (13.5 ounce size)
Vegetable stock as needed

Sort through the lentils and remove any discolored or half-lentils.

Pour the water, 1 tablespoon salt, and the lentils into a big soup pot. Mix all the dry spices together in a small bowl; then add 2½ tablespoons of the spice mix to the soup pot, reserving the rest.

Bring to a boil, reduce heat and simmer for 1 hour. Lentils should be soft, but not mushy. Drain the lentils in a colander and set aside.

In a large pot or Dutch oven heat the oil over medium heat until shimmering. Add the onions and garlic and cook for 5 minutes until soft. Stir in the celery and carrots and cook for an additional 10 minutes. Add the reserved spice mixture, stirring well for 1–2 minutes. Add the tomato paste and stir in to soften for 2 minutes. Stir in the coconut milk and reduce heat to low, cooking for 3–5 minutes. Add cooked lentils in batches, allowing the mixture to thicken. If you desire a bit more broth add vegetable stock to taste. Add salt to taste. Serve hot.

MEAT DISHES

Meat was a treat for my family when I was growing up. I remember my mother serving rice pilau, rich with spices and savory potatoes, dotted with small pieces of beef, goat, or chicken. In Kenya, unless you have a lot of money, you may only eat meat on Fridays, holidays, or at weddings or religious celebrations, although marinated, spicy kebabs are a common sight as street food all over Africa. I credit the chefs I worked with for introducing me to the many ways meat can be prepared and served. These chef mentors encouraged me to experiment and create recipes that incorporate familiar ingredients from East Africa and spice combinations and herbs from around the world. I particularly love jerk seasonings and appreciate how Caribbean spices have opened up opportunities for me to create new meat recipes.

MOROCCAN SPICE CHICKEN KEBABS

Active Prep Time: 45 minutes–1 hour
Inactive Prep Time: 6–8 hours
Cook Time: 25–30 minutes
Serves: 6–8

Ingredients:
2–3 pounds boneless organic chicken breasts
1 tablespoon curry powder
2 tablespoons fresh ginger, chopped fine
1½ tablespoons ground cinnamon
1 tablespoon ground coriander
1 tablespoon smoked paprika
½ tablespoon ground allspice
1 tablespoon dried thyme
2 tablespoons dried parsley
1 tablespoon kosher salt
1 teaspoon brown sugar
2 tablespoons rice wine vinegar
1 cup olive oil
Bamboo skewers

Begin 6–8 hours in advance for proper marinating time. Cut the chicken into 2-inch cubes and set aside in a medium to large bowl.

In a food processor or blender add all the spices, sugar, and vinegar. Run on low and add the olive oil slowly until all the ingredients are combined and a paste forms. With a rubber spatula, scoop the spice paste into the bowl of chicken cubes. Mix the chicken and spices by hand until the chicken is well coated. Cover with plastic wrap and put in the refrigerator for 6–8 hours.

About 15 minutes before cook time, place the skewers in a pan of water and set aside. Remove the chicken from refrigerator and place chicken cubes onto the skewers. Cubes may be touching slightly.

You can use either a nonstick pan or a grill.

On the stove: Heat a little oil in the nonstick pan over medium heat. Cook the kebabs between 6–8 minutes, turning them to brown on all sides.

On the grill: Cook the kebabs for 7–10 minutes, turning to brown on all sides.

KENYAN BEEF KEBABS

Active Prep Time: 45 minutes to 1 hour
Inactive Prep Time: 6–8 hours
Cook Time: 30 minutes
Serves: 6–8

Ingredients:
2–3 pounds beef
2 tablespoons fresh ginger, peeled and minced
1 tablespoon ground coriander
1 tablespoon ground cumin
½ tablespoon cayenne pepper
1 tablespoon ground rosemary
2 tablespoons dried thyme
1 tablespoon ground cinnamon
1 tablespoon kosher salt
1–1½ cups olive oil
Bamboo skewers

Begin 6–8 hours in advance for proper marinating time. Cut the beef into 2-inch cubes and set aside in a medium to large bowl.

In a food processor or blender add all the spices. Run on low, adding the olive oil slowly until all the spices are combined and a paste forms. With a rubber spatula scoop the spice paste into the bowl of beef cubes. Mix the beef and spices by hand till the beef is well coated. Cover with plastic wrap and place in the refrigerator for 6–8 hours.

About 15 minutes before cook time, place the skewers in a pan of water. Remove beef marinade from refrigerator. Place beef cubes onto the skewers. Cubes may be touching slightly.

Cook the kebabs in a nonstick pan on the stove or on a grill.

On the stove: Place pan over medium heat and add a bit of oil. Cook the kebabs for about 5–8 minutes, turning the kebabs to brown on all sides.

On the grill: Cook the kebabs for 7–10 minutes, turning to brown on all sides.

PISTACHIO CRUSTED CURRIED CHICKEN

Prep Time: 30 minutes
Inactive Prep Time: 2 hours.
Cook Time: 20–30 minutes
Serves: 4–6

Ingredients:
2 pounds chicken breast cut crosswise into thin slices
4 cups water
2 teaspoons salt
2 tablespoons sugar
1½ cups pistachios, roasted, and salted
½ cup bread crumbs
2 tablespoons curry powder or hot curry powder
2 tablespoons dried parsley
½ teaspoon salt (only if using unsalted pistachios)
1 or 2 eggs
½ cup olive oil for cooking

In a large bowl or container combine the water, salt, and sugar to create a brine. Place the chicken slices in the brine, cover and refrigerate for 2 hours.

After chicken is brined, drain the chicken pieces and pat dry with paper towels. Place in a bowl and set aside.

Preheat oven to 200 degrees and put a cookie sheet covered in foil inside. Combine the remaining ingredients in a food processor, pulse until everything is crushed, and transfer to a large flat-bottom container, set aside. In a medium-sized bowl beat the eggs and set aside.

In a large nonstick frying pan add some oil and heat over medium heat until shimmering. In batches, dip the chicken in the egg wash, coating both sides. Then dip the chicken in the pistachio mixture, coating both sides. Transfer to the hot pan and cook 2 to 3 minutes on each side. Place cooked chicken in the oven on the cookie sheet to keep warm until served.

GOAT PILAU

Prep Time: 30–45 minutes
Cook Time: 3 hours
Serves: 4–6

Ingredients for the goat stock:
2 pounds goat with bones, cut into 1½" cubes
½ teaspoon freshly ground black pepper
1 tablespoon salt
6 cups water

Over high heat bring the goat, pepper, salt, and water to a boil. Cook at a tender boil for 1½ hours. Remove goat from stock and set aside. Reserve 4 cups of the goat stock.

Ingredients for the spice mix:
12 green cardamom pods or 1¾ teaspoons ground green cardamom
1 teaspoon cumin seeds or 1 teaspoon ground cumin
1 teaspoon coriander seeds or 1 teaspoon ground coriander
5 cinnamon sticks or 2½ teaspoons ground cinnamon

Place the ingredients in a mortar and add a bit of oil. Work the spices with a pestle until everything is crushed and melded together. Using a mortar and pestle is traditional. Feel free to use pre-ground spices if you prefer.

Ingredients for the pilau:
1 cup olive oil
1 large red onion, diced
5 cloves garlic, minced
2 tablespoons tomato paste
4 Roma tomatoes, diced
1 large carrot, peeled and thinly sliced
6–8 medium red potatoes, peeled and quartered
2 cups basmati rice
4 cups goat stock

In a 4½ quart or larger Dutch oven or comparable heavy-bottom pot heat the oil over medium heat until shimmering. Sauté onion and garlic until softened, about 5 minutes. Turn the heat to low, add the spice mixture and cook for 5 minutes until the spices start to stick to the bottom of the pot. Add the tomato paste and mix well, cooking for 1 minute. Add tomatoes, carrots, and potatoes mixing well, then simmer for 5–7 minutes.

(continued on next page)

Add the rice and the goat cubes, including the bones for a traditional flair. Mix well, coating the rice and the goat. Pour in 4 cups of goat stock.

Increase heat to medium-high and bring to a boil. Turn to low heat, cover and simmer for 30–40 minutes. The rice should be cooked and the juice gone.

You can also cook the pilau in the oven. Bring the mixture to a boil and then place your Dutch oven or heavy casserole dish in the oven and cook at 300 degrees for 30–50 minutes.

SLOW ROASTED HARISSA LEG OF LAMB

Prep Time: 20–30 minutes
Cook Time: 2½–3 hours
Serves: 6–8

Ingredients:
2–3 pounds leg of lamb
6 cloves garlic, peeled
8 whole cloves
2 tablespoons Harissa spice mix (see page 34)
1 tablespoon salt
3 tablespoons olive oil
4–6 bay leaves

Preheat oven to 200 degrees. Place a sheet of aluminum foil lengthwise in a large baking dish and another sheet crosswise. Put the leg of lamb on the foil. Poke 6 holes in the lamb with a knife. Place garlic in the holes and stud the meat with the cloves.

Place the Harissa spice mix in a small bowl with the salt and olive oil, creating a loose paste. Rub the paste all over the lamb and place bay leaves on top. Wrap the foil around the leg of lamb like a cocoon.

Roast the lamb for 2½ to 3 hours until the internal temperature reaches 145 degrees, medium rare. Remove from the oven and let rest for an hour. Place on a serving dish and pour the pan drippings reserved in the tinfoil back onto the lamb.

Serve with fresh Mango Ginger Chutney (see page 73).

BAHARAT SPICE BURGER WITH CARAMELIZED FENNEL

Prep Time: 15–20 minutes
Inactive Prep Time: 2 hours
Cook Time: 1 hour
Serves: 4–6

Ingredients:
2 pounds ground beef
2–3 tablespoons Baharat Spice Blend (see page 34)
1 to 1½ tablespoons dried parsley
2 tablespoons olive oil plus 1 teaspoon
1 bulb fennel (or 1 onion)
½ teaspoon salt
Freshly cracked black pepper to taste
Feta cheese for six burgers, to taste
Burger bun or sourdough bread

Create a paste with the Baharat Spice Blend, parsley, and 2 tablespoons of olive oil. Place the beef in a medium to large bowl and fold the spice mixture into the ground beef with your hands. Cover with plastic wrap and place in the refrigerator for 2 hours.

Trim the ends of the fennel and slice the bulb into strips. Heat a medium-sized frying pan with 1 teaspoon of olive oil over medium heat until shimmering. Add the fennel and stir to coat with the oil. Add the salt and pepper and reduce the heat to low. Cook for up to 45 minutes, stirring occasionally, until the fennel softens. The fennel may turn a light brown in color.

Form the ground beef into 6 patties. Fire up your grill and cook the burgers to the desired doneness. Add the feta at the last minute and let it soften slightly. Place burgers on buns and top with caramelized fennel. Serve hot!

Serve with Cassava Fries, see page 65.

As a lark, make some Harissa Ketchup by combining ½ cup of ketchup and ½ tablespoon of Harissa spice mixture.

Fabulous Fennel
Fennel is known for its distinctive licorice smell and taste when raw. If you don't like licorice, don't worry. When fennel is cooked the overt licorice taste disappears, resulting in a treat that has a slightly more textured consistency and a light and fresh flavor compared to caramelized onions. Give it a try, you'll like it!

CINNAMON SMOKED PAPRIKA SLOW ROASTED BEEF BRISKET

Active Prep Time: 20–30 minutes
Inactive Prep Time: 8–24 hours
Cook Time: 3–3½ hours
Serves: 4–6

Ingredients for the marinade:
4 pounds beef brisket
½–¾ cup olive oil
3 tablespoons sweet smoked paprika
2 tablespoons ground cinnamon
1 teaspoon allspice
1½ tablespoons coriander
1 tablespoon dried rosemary, crushed or ground
1 teaspoon dried thyme
1 tablespoon salt
1 teaspoon freshly cracked black pepper
½ teaspoon cayenne
6 whole cloves

Ingredients for the sauce:
1 medium to large yellow or red onion, chopped fine
1 tablespoon garlic, minced
1 tablespoon tomato paste
4 bay leaves
1 cup red wine
1 cup beef stock
1 cup chicken stock

In a large bowl mix the olive oil with the dry spices to create a paste and set aside.

Trim the majority of the fat off the brisket, leaving a bit for cooking. Place the brisket in the bowl and rub the spice mixture into the meat. Cover and refrigerate for 8 to 24 hours.

Preheat the oven to 250 degrees. Place 2 tablespoons of olive oil in a medium to large saucepan and when shimmering add the onion and garlic, cooking until softened, about 3–5 minutes. Add the tomato paste and mix well for 1 minute. Add the bay leaves and wine and cook on medium heat for an additional 3 minutes. Finally, pour in the chicken and beef stock and simmer for 15 minutes, reducing the liquid by about a third.

Put a bit of olive oil in a cast iron skillet over medium-high heat until the oil is shimmering. Sear the brisket on all sides using tongs to turn the meat. Place the brisket in a roasting dish and pour the wine/stock sauce over it. Roast in the oven for 2½ to 3 hours until the internal temperature is 175 degrees. Remove from the oven, cover with foil and let rest until the internal temperature is 185 degrees.

FISH

Africans like their fish crispy, even dry by American standards. Working at The Fish Cellar in New York, I discovered that I didn't know everything there was to know about cooking fish. There, I learned to prepare the shrimp, crab and fish I was so familiar with, cooking it completely, but gently, leaving it soft and moist, so it could absorb flavors, spices and sauces. This approach has allowed me to develop recipes using familiar spices from home, as well as herbs and spices from other cultures. I grew up with fish, and every time I prepare a new recipe or offer an old favorite at Jambo, I want people to say, "This is the best fish I ever had."

PECAN ENCRUSTED SALMON

Prep Time: 10–15 minutes
Cook Time: 10–12 minutes
Serves: 4–6

Ingredients:
2 pounds salmon, skin on one side
1 cup pecan pieces
2 tablespoons dried parsley
1 tablespoon smoked sweet paprika
1 teaspoon coriander
1 teaspoon curry powder
½ teaspoon cinnamon powder
½ teaspoon ground black pepper
½ teaspoon salt
Olive oil for cooking

Slice the salmon into four 6-ounce portions and set aside on a plate or baking sheet.

Combine the remaining ingredients in a food processor until mixed thoroughly. Transfer the mixture to a flat-bottomed glass pan or a baking sheet with sides.

Add some olive oil to a large nonstick skillet and cook on high heat until shimmering. In the meantime, dredge the fleshy side of each piece of salmon in the pecan mixture. Place salmon skin side down in the pan and reduce heat to medium. Cook for 7 minutes. Flip and cook for an additional 3 minutes until salmon is medium. It should feel firm to the touch or have an inside temperature of 120–125 degrees.

Serve hot with Ginger-Rum Sweet Potatoes (see page 80).

SWAHILI SHRIMP PILAU

Pilau is a traditional dish that is similar to an East Indian biryani.

Prep Time: 30–40 minutes
Cook Time: 1 hour
Serves: 4–6

Ingredients for the spice mix:
1 teaspoon cumin seed or 1 teaspoon ground cumin
1 teaspoon coriander seed or 1 teaspoon ground coriander
12 green cardamom pods or 1¾ teaspoons ground green cardamom
4 cinnamon sticks or 2 teaspoons ground cinnamon
5 whole cloves or ½ teaspoon ground cloves
½ teaspoon ground black pepper
½ teaspoon salt

If using whole ingredients combine them in mortar (bowl) and add a dash of olive oil to moisten the spices. With a pestle work the mixture until it is crushed and melded together. Crushing spices with mortar and pestle is traditional, but feel free to use ground ingredients if you desire.

Ingredients for the pilau:
½ cup olive oil
1 medium red onion, diced
4 garlic cloves, minced
2 jalapeños, diced
1 medium red bell pepper, diced
1 teaspoon fresh ginger, minced
2 tablespoons tomato paste
4 medium Roma tomatoes, diced
1 or 2 carrots, peeled and thinly sliced
4 medium red potatoes, peeled and diced medium
2 cups basmati rice
2 cups vegetable stock
2 cups chicken stock
Salt to taste

1–1½ pounds medium shrimp, peeled and deveined

In a 4½ quart or larger Dutch oven (or comparable heavy-bottomed pot), heat the olive oil over medium heat until shimmering and cook the onion and garlic for 2 minutes. Add the peppers and ginger and cook for an additional 3 minutes. Turn the heat to low and add the spice mixture, cooking until the spices start to stick to the bottom of the pot, about 5 minutes. Stir in the tomato paste and mix well, cooking for 1 minute. Add the tomatoes, carrots, and potatoes, mixing well; simmer for 5–7 minutes.

Stir in the rice, mixing until it is thoroughly coated. Pour in the vegetable and chicken stock.

Increase heat to medium-high and bring to a boil. Reduce heat to low, cover and simmer for 30–35 minutes. The rice should be cooked and the juice gone. You can also cook this in the oven. Bring the mixture to a boil and place in your Dutch oven at 300 degrees for 30–50 minutes.

While the pilau is cooking, season the shrimp with fresh black pepper and salt and set aside. Once the pilau is cooked, heat some olive oil in a large skillet on medium-low heat until it is shimmering. Cook the shrimp in batches or all at once, turning them over as they become pink, no more than 2–3 minutes per side. Once cooked, toss the shrimp with the pilau mixture and serve hot.

PILI PILI SHRIMP WITH COCONUT SAUCE

Inactive Prep Time: 1 hour
Active Prep Time: 45 minutes–1 hour
Cook Time: 45 minutes for the sauce
Serves: 6–8

Ingredients:
3 pounds shrimp (16–20 per pound), fresh or frozen fresh

Ingredients for the Pili Pili spice paste:
2–3 African bird's eye chilis, dried
1 tablespoon crushed garlic
1 tablespoon coriander
1 tablespoon paprika powder
3 tablespoons fresh lemon juice
1 tablespoon brown sugar
1–2 tablespoons ground cayenne*
½ teaspoon crushed black pepper
1 tablespoon kosher salt
1½ cups blended olive oil

Ingredients for the coconut sauce:
1 small yellow onion, diced
½ cup blended olive oil
3 cloves chopped garlic
2 tablespoons tomato paste
6 medium Roma tomatoes, diced
1 can coconut milk (13.5 ounces)
1 cup vegetable stock

Peel and devein shrimp. Lightly coat them with garlic, salt, and olive oil, and place in a large bowl. Set aside.

To make Pili Pili, use a food processor or blender to combine all spices from chiles to salt. While running the blender on low, slowly add olive oil until the mixture turns into a paste. Set aside. *If you already have paste made, use 3 tablespoons for this recipe.*

Heat oil in a large saucepan over medium heat until shimmering. Add onions and garlic and sauté with a wooden spoon until soft, about 3–5 minutes. Stir in Pili Pili spice paste cooking for 3–4 minutes or until spices start to stick to the pot. Mix in tomato paste, stirring well and cooking for 2 minutes. Add diced tomato and let simmer for 3–5 minutes until spices loosen from the bottom of pot. Pour in coconut milk and vegetable stock, mixing well.

Turn the heat to medium high and slowly bring to a boil, cooking for 8–10 minutes. Turn heat down to medium and simmer for 25 minutes, stirring occasionally. Remove from heat and set aside.

Heat a large frying pan over medium heat and add a bit of olive oil. Add shrimp and cook for 3–5 minutes, turning shrimp over midway to cook both sides. Combine shrimp and sauce and serve hot over rice.

2 tablespoons of cayenne will result in a very spicy hot sauce which is wonderful. If you don't like a lot of heat, reduce the cayenne to 1 tablespoon.

WHITE CORN MEAL ENCRUSTED DOVER SOLE

Prep Time: 15 minutes
Cook Time: Up to 30 minutes
Serves: 4–6

Ingredients:
2 pounds Dover sole or tilapia filets
1 cup white corn meal
1 tablespoon dried parsley
½ teaspoon ground black pepper
½ teaspoon salt
½ cup olive oil for cooking

Combine the cornmeal, parsley, pepper and salt in a flat-bottomed dish and mix well. Heat ¼ cup of oil in a medium-sized, nonstick pan over medium heat until the oil is shimmering. Dip a filet of fish into the corn meal mixture and transfer to the frying pan. Cook in batches 2–3 minutes on one side. Flip with a silicon spatula and repeat on the other side for 2–3 minutes. The fish should be white and flaky. Add more oil and repeat the frying process for the rest of the fish.

You can also use tilapia. If you use tilapia increase the cooking time to 4–5 minutes each side.

SPICED MARINATED ROCK FISH IN CORN HUSKS

Active Prep Time: 30 minutes
Inactive Prep Time: 1–4 hours
Cook Time: 20 minutes
Serves: 4

Ingredients:
2 pounds rock fish or red snapper
¼ cup olive oil
1 tablespoon garlic, minced
1 jalapeño, deseeded and minced
¼ cup fresh scallions, chopped
½ teaspoon fresh ginger, minced
1 tablespoon coriander
1 teaspoon smoked sweet paprika
4 whole cloves
½ teaspoon salt
½ teaspoon freshly ground black pepper
4–5 dried corn husks

Soak the corn husks in room temperature water in a large pan or bowl for 10 minutes to soften. Once they are softened, drain them and set aside.

Clean the fish, removing any bones, and cut the fish into 3-inch pieces. Place the fish in a large bowl and set aside. In a food processor mix together the oil, garlic, pepper, scallions, and all spices, transforming them into a paste. Coat the fish with the spice paste mixture and set aside in the refrigerator for an hour.

Open the softened husks gently and place them on a baking sheet. Place the pieces of fish inside the center of the husks. Fold the husks over to enclose the fish inside creating little packets and set aside.

Bring water to a boil in the bottom part of a steamer unit. Arrange the husks in the steamer basket, ensuring that the fish stays inside. Steam on low heat for 8–10 minutes. If you don't have a steamer basket, use a sauté pan. Place water in the bottom, arrange the husks, cover with a lid and cook 8–10 minutes.

Serve hot with Green Mango Chutney (see page 71) and basmati rice.

BANANA LEAF-WRAPPED ISLAND-SPICED MAHI MAHI WITH TAMARIND COCONUT SAUCE

As featured on *Diners, Drive-ins and Dives*

Active Prep Time: 2 hours
Inactive Prep Time: 2 hours
Cook Time: 1¼ hours
Serves: 6–8

Ingredients for the marinade:
4 pounds fresh mahi mahi
3 jalapeños, deseeded and chopped fine
3 tablespoons fresh ginger, peeled and minced
3 tablespoons red pepper flakes
2 tablespoons chili powder
2 tablespoons paprika
1 tablespoon ground allspice
1 tablespoon light brown sugar
1 tablespoon ground coriander
1 tablespoon ground cumin
1 tablespoon fresh garlic, minced
1 tablespoon kosher salt
½ teaspoon freshly ground black pepper
1½ cups olive oil
8 banana leaves

Ingredients for the sauce:
2½ cups tamarind juice, squeezed from tamarind pulp
¼ cup olive oil
1 small yellow onion, diced
5–6 cloves garlic, minced
1 tablespoon ground coriander
1 tablespoon ground cumin
1 tablespoon curry powder
1 tablespoon dried thyme
2 cups ripe mango, peeled, deseeded, and diced
1 can coconut milk (13.5 ounces)
1½ tablespoons kosher salt
½ tablespoon freshly ground black pepper

Cut the mahi mahi into 6-inch portions and set aside in a bowl. Place all marinade ingredients, except for the oil, in a food processor. With the processor running, add the oil slowly until a paste forms. Transfer the marinade to a small bowl and gently coat the mahi mahi with the marinade. Lay a banana leaf flat on a small baking sheet and wipe it with a wet, warm towel. Lay a piece of fish on the leaf and fold the leaf over. Repeat with the remaining leaves and fish. Cover with plastic wrap and chill in the refrigerator for 2 hours.

While the fish is marinating, prepare the sauce. First, place the tamarind pulp in a bowl of warm water and let soften 3–5 minutes. Then, squeeze the tamarind until the water turns brown. Measure 2½ cups of tamarind juice and set aside.

In a large saucepan bring the olive oil to shimmering over high heat. Add the onion and garlic, cooking until soft, about 3 minutes. Add the coriander, cumin, curry, and thyme, and cook until the spices start to stick to the pot, about 3 minutes. Add the mango and stir until spices loosen; then stir in the tamarind juice and coconut milk. Reduce heat to medium–high and cook 8–10 minutes. Reduce heat to medium–low, add the salt and pepper, and cook for 20–25 minutes, stirring occasionally. When the sauce has reduced 25%, remove from heat and set aside. Bring water in a steamer pan to boil. Add the fish in the banana leaves to the steamer and steam until the juices turn white, between 10–15 minutes. Remove from steamer with tongs and cut each banana leaf in half. Keep fish in the banana leaves, plate, and pour some sauce over each serving.

Serve hot with rice or any other starch.

This dish can also be made using tilapia.

PAPAYA HABAÑERO MARINATED GRILLED SWORDFISH

Active Prep Time: 15 minutes
Inactive Prep Time: 2 hours
Cook Time: 10–15 minutes
Serves: 4–6

Ingredients:
2 pounds swordfish
1 habañero pepper, deseeded and minced
1 teaspoon fresh garlic, minced
2 tablespoons fresh cilantro, chopped
Juice from half a lemon
1½ cups medium–ripe papaya, pitted, skinned, and chopped
½ teaspoon salt
¼ teaspoon ground black pepper
1 tablespoon olive oil
Olive oil for cooking

Cut the swordfish into 6-ounce pieces and place them in a large bowl. Using an immersion blender or a regular blender, puree the papaya chunks with the rest of the ingredients for 1–2 minutes and place in a large bowl. Pour the spice mixture over the fish, cover, and place in the refrigerator for 2 hours.

Heat a grill or large skillet to medium heat. Brush the grill with some oil or place a bit in the bottom of the skillet. Grill the fish 4–5 minutes on each side.

Serve hot with a side of Coconut Basmati Rice and Sautéed Spinach (see page 83 and 81).

How to Choose a Papaya
1. Look for a mostly yellow with a bit of green fruit and allow to ripen 2–3 days at home. A fully ripe papaya is bright yellow.
2. Papaya fruit should feel firm and heavy for its size. It should yield slightly to a gentle touch.
3. Avoid fruit that has blemishes, soft spots or is overly soft.
4. Choose a papaya with a light sweet smell by sniffing the base where the fruit was attached to the tree.

SWEETS

In Kenya, desserts are not typically a separate course. Sweets are served as an integral part of the meal, along with the rest of the food. As a child, the sweets, which might be a pudding or pancake and sometimes even a cake, appeared at the same time as the rice or *ugali*, with its sauce, and the fish or other protein. If you wanted to eat the sweet first, that's what you did. Traditional Swahili sweets recipes often include an element of spiciness and regularly feature fruits like mango, coconut, and pineapple.

VITU VANGANU WITH CARDAMOM

Prep Time: 15 minutes
Cook Time: 20–30 minutes
Serves: 6–8

Ingredients for the dough:
2 cups flour
2 tablespoons sugar
1 teaspoon ground green cardamom
1 teaspoon baking powder
1 egg
¼ cup salted butter, melted
¼ cup warm water (if needed)

Ingredients for the simple syrup:
½ cup water
¾ cup sugar
½ teaspoon ground green cardamom

2 cups grape seed or other high heat oil for frying

In a large bowl, whisk together the flour, sugar, cardamom, baking powder, and egg. Begin mixing the dough with your hands and slowly add the melted butter. Initially, the dough may stick to your hands. If the dough is very dry, add some warm water. Knead the dough until the texture is similar to bread dough and it stops sticking to your hands.

Roll out the dough on a floured surface to a ½–1-inch thickness. Cut into 1-inch strips. Then cut the strips into 1½-inch lengths on a diagonal to create diamond shapes and set aside.

In a large skillet heat the oil to 375 degrees. Fry the dough until golden, about 3 minutes. The dough should be crispy. Drain on paper towels.

To make the syrup, combine the sugar, water, and cardamom in a medium-sized pan and heat on low until sugar is melted.

Toss the crispy dough with the sugar syrup until it is coated. Garnish with a bit more cardamom if desired.

Serve hot with coffee or tea. Vitu Vanganu also makes a great traveling snack.

COCONUT CARDAMOM RICE CAKE

Prep Time: 9 hours
Cook Time: 20 minutes
Serves: 4

Ingredients:
1 cup basmati rice
1 cup coconut milk
½ cup sugar
1 teaspoon ground green cardamom
1 teaspoon yeast
2 egg whites

Soak the rice in water for at least 8 hours. Drain.

Preheat oven to 350 degrees. Place rice and all other ingredients into a blender and blend on medium for 10–15 minutes nonstop. Pour the mixture into a large bowl and cover with a clean cloth or kitchen towel. Let rise for about 20–30 minutes.

Put an 8-inch nonstick cake pan over low heat on a stovetop burner. Once the pan is warm, pour the rice mixture into the pan and cook for 5 minutes to brown the bottom of the rice cake. Transfer the cake pan to the oven.

Bake for 15 minutes. The rice cake should be firm and golden brown. If not, cook an additional 5 minutes.

COCONUT CHOCOLATE BREAD PUDDING

Prep Time: 40 minutes
Cook Time: 1¾ hours
Serves: 6–8

Ingredients for the bread pudding:
1 loaf challah bread
3 tablespoons butter, melted
3 cups half and half
1 cup whole milk
1 vanilla bean, cut in half
8 ounces semi-sweet chocolate chips or chunks
1 cup sugar
4 whole eggs
4 egg yolks
Pinch salt
1 cup sweetened coconut flakes

Ingredients for the coconut cinnamon sugar sauce:
1 can coconut milk (13.5 ounces)
½ tablespoon ground cinnamon
½ cup sugar
½ teaspoon vanilla extract (optional)

Preheat oven to 350 degrees. Cut the challah into thick slices and then dice into large chunks. Place the bread chunks on a rimmed baking sheet and crisp in the oven for 12–15 minutes, turning the chunks over half way through.

In a medium-sized saucepan, combine the butter, half and half, milk, vanilla bean, and chocolate, and cook over low heat until the chocolate melts and the mixture is warm. Remove from heat. In a large bowl beat together the eggs, egg yolks, and sugar. Stir in the salt and coconut, then fold the milk mixture into the egg mixture. Toss in the toasted bread chunks to coat them evenly.

Evenly spread the bread mixture on the bottom of a buttered baking dish. Cover with an oven safe lid or tinfoil and bake for 90 minutes. Remove from oven and let cool slightly.

Combine the coconut milk, cinnamon, sugar, and vanilla in a small saucepan and cook over low to medium heat until warm. Pour over baked bread mixture.

Serve warm.

COCONUT RUM BLACK RICE PUDDING

Prep Time: 15 minutes
Cook time: 60 minutes
Serves: 4–6

Ingredients:
1 cup black rice
1 teaspoon salt
3 cups half and half
½ cup rum
¼ teaspoon ground cloves
½ teaspoon ground nutmeg
½ teaspoon ground allspice
1 tablespoon ground cinnamon
1 can coconut milk (13.5 ounces)
½ cup shredded coconut
½–1 cup honey to taste
Whipped cream

In a large-sized saucepan bring 2 cups of water to boil with 1 teaspoon salt. Add the rice and cook until soft but not mushy, about 30 minutes.

Pour the half and half and rum into the saucepan with the rice. Add the cloves, nutmeg, allspice, and cinnamon. Bring to a boil, reduce heat and simmer until thickened, 15–25 minutes. Stir in the coconut milk and shredded coconut.

Bring back to a boil and simmer for another 5 minutes. Remove from heat, stir in honey to desired sweetness.

Serve warm or chilled with fresh whipped cream.

MKATE WA MAJI STUFFED WITH TROPICAL FRUIT

Prep Time: 30 minutes
Cook Time: 25 minutes
Serves: 6–8

Ingredients:
1 ripe mango, peeled, pitted, and cut into small chunks
1 banana, peeled, halved and sliced
1 pineapple, peeled, cored, and cut into small chunks
1 pint strawberries, destemmed and cut into halves or quarters
Zest from one lemon
Juice from one lemon
1 cup water
¾ cup flour
1 tablespoon sugar
1 egg
Pinch of salt
Whipped cream

Prep the fruit and place in a large bowl. Add the lemon zest and juice and mix together gently. Set aside.

In a medium bowl combine the water, flour, sugar, egg, and salt to create a batter. Heat a nonstick pan to medium heat. With a small ladle scoop out batter onto the pan, twisting the pan so the batter spreads evenly over the bottom, forming a crepe. When the rim of the crepe begins to dry and brown, use a silicone or rubber spatula to flip it over. Cook until golden, remove from heat, and set aside. Repeat process until batter is gone.

To serve, place a crepe on a plate, fill one side with the fruit mixture, fold the crepe over, and top with whipped cream.

GRILLED PINEAPPLE WITH VANILLA ICE CREAM AND HONEY

Prep Time: 20 minutes
Inactive Prep Time: 45 minutes
Cook Time: 45 minutes
Serves: 6–8

Ingredients:
1 fresh pineapple, peeled, cored, and sliced
½ tablespoon cinnamon
½ cup rum
1 teaspoon honey per serving
Vanilla ice cream

Peel the pineapple with a sharp knife. Cut the pineapple into ½-inch rings. Then, core the center of each ring with a pineapple corer or paring knife. Place the pineapple in a bowl, toss with the cinnamon, and pour in the rum. Let sit 45 minutes.

Preheat oven to 350 degrees. Place the pineapple rings in a single layer on a baking dish and bake in the oven until the pineapple is caramelized, about 45 minutes.

Remove from oven and let cool about 2 minutes. While warm, place pineapple rings in separate dessert plates or bowls, top with vanilla ice cream, and drizzle with honey.

Learn how to pick the perfect pineapple. See page 75 for instructions.

DRINKS

I grew up drinking chai every day. It was the "have-to" drink, either black or with milk. Kenyan tea is world famous, and mixed with Indian spices like ginger, cinnamon, and cardamom, chai might be the original fusion drink. We always drank chai hot, at home in the mornings or in a small restaurant or hotel for an afternoon break. I had never seen iced tea or iced chai until I came to the United States and was truly amazed that anyone would want to drink cold tea. The cold, iced drinks we loved growing up were fruit-based—tamarind, mango, or passion fruit juices—freshly squeezed and available at kiosks or stands.

SPICED CINNAMON TEA

Active Prep Time: 5 minutes
Inactive Prep Time: 2–6 hours
Cook Time: 20 minutes
Serves: 4–6

Ingredients:
2 tablespoons loose black tea
2 tablespoons ground black cardamom
1 tablespoon ginger powder
1 teaspoon cinnamon
1 teaspoon freshly ground black pepper
4–6 cups water
½ cup sweetener of your choice

Place all ingredients in a medium-sized saucepan and bring to a boil. Reduce heat and simmer 15–20 minutes. Add the sweetener of your choice, stirring until dissolved. Remove from heat, cover, and let stand 2–6 hours for flavors to meld. Strain mixture to remove any solids if desired. Reheat and serve hot.

MANGO GINGER LEMONADE

Active Prep Time: 20 minutes
Inactive Prep Time: 1 hour
Serves: 4–6

Ingredients:
4 fresh mangoes, peeled, deseeded, and cut into cubes
½ cup fresh ginger root, peeled and chopped
Juice of 4 fresh lemons
6 cups water
Sweetener of your choice to taste

Puree the mangoes and ginger in a blender. Add the lemon juice and pulse a few times. Pour into a large glass pitcher with the water and stir with a wooden spoon to mix well. Add sweetener to taste, stirring well. Place in the refrigerator to chill, about 1 hour.

Serve cold with a lemon slice.

CARDAMOM TAMARIND JUICE

Active Prep Time: 15 minutes
Inactive Prep Time: 8–10 hours
Serves: 4–6

Ingredients:
3 ounces wet tamarind, seedless
8 cups warm water
1 cup light brown sugar
2 tablespoons ground green cardamom

Place the warm water and tamarind in a large-sized saucepan. Let the tamarind soak for 3–5 minutes. Squeeze the tamarind with your hands until the water turns brown. Discard leftover tamarind pulp. Add sugar and cardamom and bring to a boil for 3–5 minutes.

Remove from heat and let sit for 8 hours. Pour into a pitcher or glass jar and refrigerate until cold. Serve chilled.

HIBISCUS COOLER

Active Prep Time: 10 minutes
Inactive Prep Time: Up to 12 hours
Cook Time: 7–10 minutes
Serves: 4–6

Ingredients:
6 cups water
½ cup dried hibiscus flowers
½ teaspoon ground cloves
½ cup fresh ginger, peeled and cut into slices
¼ to ½ cup brown sugar to taste

Place all ingredients in a large-sized saucepan and bring to a boil. Reduce heat and simmer for 3–5 minutes. Strain to remove ginger and hibiscus and discard solids.

Pour into a glass pitcher or jar and refrigerate for 8–12 hours. Serve chilled.

JAMBO CAFÉ CHAI

Active Prep Time: 10 minutes
Inactive Prep Time: None or up to 8 hours
Serves: 4–6

Ingredients:
3 cups water
2 tablespoons black tea
½ tablespoon ginger powder
1 tablespoon ground green cardamom
1 teaspoon ground cinnamon
½ teaspoon ground allspice
½ teaspoon ground nutmeg
½ teaspoon freshly cracked black pepper
3 cups milk
Sweetener of your choice

Bring the water and spices to a boil in a large-sized saucepan. Reduce heat to low, add milk, and simmer for 3–5 minutes, stirring occasionally. Remove from heat and let sit for 5 minutes. Add a sweetener of your choice. Chai is ready to drink.

For best results, allow the chai to cool and place in a glass jar in the refrigerator for 8 hours.

Reheat and serve hot and sweeten to taste.

GLOSSARY

African Bird's Eye chili: a hot Chili native to Africa, growing both wild and domesticated. It is sometimes referred to as *Piri Piri* or *Pili Pili*.

Arrowroot Powder: a starch obtained from various tropical plants. It can be used as a substitute for corn starch.

Baharat: a spice blend typically used in Middle Eastern cuisine. Baharat means "spices."

Bajun: The Bajun are located primarily in the district of Lamu, Kenya on the coast of the Indian Ocean. They occupy the tiny island of Lamu, just north of the Tana River. This small island is less than ten miles long and four miles wide. They are also reported to live in Tanzania.

Banana Leaves: large, flexible, waterproof leaves used for cooking in many cuisines, imparting a subtle sweet flavor to the food. Banana leaves used in cooking are not meant to be eaten.

Cassava Root: edible, starchy, tuberous root cultivated in tropical and sub-tropical regions. Cassava is often a staple of diets in these regions and a major source of carbohydrates. Also known as yuca, manioc, and tapioca.

Chai: a flavored tea beverage created by steeping black tea with a variety of spices or herbs. Origin is India.

Challah Bread: a braided bread of Jewish origin specifically eaten on the Sabbath and Jewish holidays.

Coconut Cream: a mixture made by simmering together four parts coconut and one part water. As its name suggests, coconut

GLOSSARY

cream is thicker, creamier, and of higher caloric content than coconut milk and is most often used in desserts.

Coconut Milk: a mixture made by simmering together equal parts coconut and water. It is typically used for curries, sauces, and stews. Coconut milk and coconut cream are not interchangeable; each will provide its own flavoring and consistency to any recipe.

Curry Powder: a term referring to a spice blend that varies widely in composition from chef to chef. While based on South Asian cuisine, curry powder and the modern use of the word curry are Western in origin.

Dawa: means medicine in Swahili, where it also means herbs.

Dhow: a traditional sailing vessel with one or two masts and lateen-rigged sails used in the Indian Ocean.

Fennel: a flowering plant species in the carrot family indigenous to the Mediterranean. In particular, Florence Fennel or *finnocchio* is the version with the bulb-like stem base that is eaten as a vegetable.

Fufu: made from cassava and/or plantains mashed to a dough-like consistency, typically eaten with stews.

Guava: a fruit cultivated in tropical and subtropical regions and belonging to the Myrtle family. Juicing results in guava nectar and is used in soups, sauces, candies, fruit bars, dried snacks and more.

Harissa: a North African chili paste or spice blend mixed with oil to make a paste.

GLOSSARY

Hibiscus: a variety of flowering plants in the Mallow family containing several hundred species native to warm-temperate, subtropical, and tropical regions throughout the world. A tea made from hibiscus flowers is common throughout the world and referred to as *bissap* in West Africa, *sorrel* in the Caribbean, and *gudhal* in India.

Jambo: a Swahili term meaning "Hello."

Jiko Stove: a charcoal-burning stove that is safer, more efficient than traditional charcoal- or wood-burning stoves.

Kangas: a rectangle of brightly colored cotton cloth with a border all around and printed with bold designs wide enough to cover you from neck to knee.

Lateen: a triangular sail set on a long yard mounted at an angle of 45 degrees to the mast.

Madawa: a mixture of "dawa" or medicine; alternatively, a pharmacy.

Mango: a juicy stone fruit native to South and Southeast Asia.

Masala: an East Indian term for a spice blend, for example *Garam Masala.*

Mchuzi: a sauce, stew, soup, or broth.

Mkate: a term part of many bread or cake recipes from East Africa which simply means bread.

Makte Wa Mufa: a cornmeal based yeast-leavened bread.

GLOSSARY

Mkate Wa Nazi: a rice flour based leavened bread with coconut.

Mishkaki: skewers of meat, in other words, a kebab.

Naan: also known as nan or Khamiri, a yeast-leavened oven-baked flatbread originating in India.

Plantain: a less sweet variety of the banana; plantains are typically eaten cooked and are usually larger, angular, and starchy.

Pilau: rice flavored with spices and stock or seasoned broth. Vegetables, poultry, fish, or meat can be added to taste.

Pili Pili: also sometimes seen spelled as *Piri Piri*. A spice blend featuring the African bird's eye chili and other spices. Also sometimes used as a synonym for an African bird's eye chili.

Ras el Hanout: a North African spice mixture. The Arabic term translates to "head of the shop" or in other words, "top shelf" to indicate that only the best spices were used in this blend. The blend is typically associated with Moroccan cuisine, but this blend has traveled to neighboring countries.

Roti: an unleavened oven-baked flatbread originating in India.

Samosa: a fried or baked pastry stuffed with a savory filling which can include potatoes, onions, peas, lentils, minced meat, and nuts, originally thought to have originated in Central Asia.

Shangazi: a Swahili term referring to one's Aunt.

Swahili: a term referring to 1) people, an ethnic group in the African Great Lakes region; 2) culture of the Swahili people;

GLOSSARY

3) a Bantu language official in Kenya, Tanzania, Uganda, and widely spoken in the Great Lakes region; and 4) a littoral region in the African Great Lakes.

Tamarind: a brown, sticky, and acidic pulp from the pod or fruit of the tamarind tree. Once ripe it is used in jams, blended into drinks, sorbets, ice creams, and other snacks.

Ugali: a dish of cornmeal, millet or sorghum flour cooked with water to form a porridge or dough. It is the most common starch featured in Swahili cooking.

Vitumbuas: a rice, cardamom and coconut treat from East African coastal countries.

WHERE TO FIND IT

Jambo Imports

Chef Ahmed Obo's African Imports store carries many specialty ingredients, including Chef Ahmed's spice blends and chutneys:

- Various Curry blends specifically designed for Chicken Curry, Lentil Stew, Sweet Potato & Black Bean Soup and Chicken Peanut Stew
- Ras el Hanout, Baharat, Harissa, Pili Pili, and Jerk blends
- Ground Allspice, Coriander, Cumin, Ginger, Smoked Sweet Paprika, Turmeric, Cinnamon, and Cayenne
- Seeds of Coriander, Cumin, Oregano, Mustard, Fennel, Anise, Cloves, and Green Cardamom
- African Bird's Eye chiles and Habaenero chiles
- Jambo Cafe Chai Mix, sweetened and unsweetened
- Hibiscus Flowers, Tamarind Paste, Tamarind Pods, and Cinnamon Sticks

Visit JamboImports.com

Finding Other Specialty Ingredients

Banana Leaves: Asian and Hispanic markets
Black Rice: Asian markets
Challah: High-end supermarkets or specialty bakers
Coconut Milk and Coconut Cream: High-end supermarkets and Asian markets
Goat: Asian and Hispanic markets
Guava: Hispanic markets in puree, nectar, paste formats
Vanilla Beans: Penzey Spices or Savory Spice shops or other online retailers

INDEX

Appetizers. See Small Plates

Apricots
Ras El Hanout Chicken and Olive Stew ...88
Moroccan Lamb Stew 91

Asparagus
Balsamic Garlic Marinated Grilled
    Asparagus..82

Avocados
Vegetable Avocado and Corn Gazpacho 53

Baharat Spice Blend *34*
Baharat Spice Burger with Caramelized
    Fennel 109

Baharat Spice Burger with Caramelized
    Fennel *109*

Balsamic Garlic Marinated Grilled
    Asparagus... *82*
Banana Leaf-Wrapped Island-Spiced Mahi
    Mahi with Tamarind Coconut Sauce... *120*

Beans
Black
Curried Black Bean and Sweet Potato
    Soup 47
Black-eyed Peas
Swahili Bajia..59
Garbanzo
Moroccan Lamb Stew 91

Lentils
Curried Lentils 98

Beef
Baharat Spice Burger with Caramelized
    Fennel 109
Cinnamon Smoked Paprika Slow Roasted
    Beef Brisket 110
Kenyan Beef Kebabs................................... 102
Slow Cooked Beef in African
    Spice Blend 95

Beverages. See Drinks

Bison
Bison Meatballs in Moroccan Spice Stew....93

Bread
Baharat Spice Burger with Caramelized
    Fennel 109
Coconut Chocolate Bread Pudding 129
Mkate wa Maji Stuffed with
    Tropical Fruit... 133
Mkate Wa Nazi 18
Mkate Wa Mufa 19
Roti...24

Cardamom Tamarind Juice *138*

Cassava
Cassava Fries..65
Cassava and Plantain Fufu 23

Cassava Fries... *65*
Cassava and Plantain Fufu *23*

INDEX

Chai
Jambo Cafe Chai 139

Cheese
Baharat Spice Burger with Caramelized Fennel 109
Coconut Goat Cheese Corn Meal 83
Curried Goat Cheese Cakes 61

Chicken
Moroccan Spice Chicken Kebabs 101
Island Spicy Peanut Coconut Chicken 89
Jambo Coconut Chicken Curry 87
Peanut Chicken Kebabs 68
Pistachio Crusted Curried Chicken 103
Ras El Hanout Chicken and Olive Stew ... 88

Chiles

African Bird's Eye Chiles
Harissa Spice Blend 34
Pili Pili Shrimp with Coconut Sauce 117
Pili Pili Spice Paste 36

Habañero
Grilled tomatillo Spiced Mango Sauce 77
Papaya Habañero Marinated Grilled Swordfish 123
Spicy coconut Guava Lime Soup 54

Jalapeño
Banana Leaf-Wrapped Island Spiced Mahi Mahi with Tamarind Coconut Sauce 120
Bison Meatballs in Moroccan Spice Stew 93
Cilantro Mango Lime Sauce 7
Green Mango Coconut Chutney 71
Mango Ginger Gazpacho 51

Plantain Fried Crab Cakes 57
Spice Marinated Rock Fish in Corn Husks 119
Swahili Bajia 59
Swahili Shrimp Pilau 114
Vegetable Avocado and Corn Gazpacho 53

Serrano
Fresh Mango and Ginger Chutney 73

Chutneys
Cilantro Mango Lime Sauce 74
Green Mango Coconut Chutney 71
Grilled tomatillo Spiced Mango Sauce 77
Fresh Mango and Ginger Chutney 73
Pineapple Coconut Rum Chutney 75

Cilantro Mango Lime Sauce 74
Cinnamon Dusted Plantains 63
Cinnamon Smoked Paprika Slow Roasted Beef Brisket 110

Coconut

Cream
Curried Mashed Red Potatoes 80
Ginger Rum Sweet Potatoes 80
Lamu Style Coconut Spinach 82
Roasted Ginger Butternut Squash Bisque 48
Spicy coconut Guava Lime Soup 54

Fresh or Flaked
Coconut Chocolate Bread Pudding 129
Coconut Rum Black Rice Pudding 131
Green Mango Coconut Chutney 71

INDEX

Mkate Wa Nazi 18
Pineapple Coconut Rum Chutney 75

<u>Milk</u>
Banana Leaf-Wrapped Island-Spiced Mahi Mahi with Tamarind Coconut Sauce 120
Coconut Basmati Rice 83
Coconut Cardamom Rice Cake 128
Coconut Chocolate Bread Pudding 129
Coconut Goat Cheese Corn Meal............... 83
Coconut Rum Black Rice Pudding.......... 131
Curried Lentils 98
Curried Black Bean and Sweet Potato Soup 47
Island Spicy Peanut Coconut Chicken 89
Jambo Coconut Chicken Curry 87
Mkate Wa Nazi 18
Pili Pili Shrimp with Coconut Sauce 117
Roasted Butternut Squash and Crab Bisque 52
Sweet Smoked Paprika Corn and Sweet Potato Soup 49

Coconut Basmati Rice 83
Coconut Cardamom Rice Cake 128
Coconut Chocolate Bread Pudding 129
Coconut Goat Cheese Corn Meal............... 83
Coconut Rum Black Rice Pudding.......... 131

Corn
Sweet Smoked Paprika Corn and Sweet Potato Soup 49
Vegetable Avocado and Corn Gazpacho 53

Corn Meal
Coconut Goat Cheese Corn Meal............... 83
Mkate Wa Nazi 18
Mkate Wa Mufa 19
Plantain Fried Crab Cakes 57
Ugali 22
White Corn Meal Encrusted Dover Sole 118

Crab
Ethiopian Spiced Seafood Gumbo 97
Roasted Butternut Squash and Crab Bisque 52
Plantain Fried Crab Cakes 57

Cucumbers
Mango Ginger Gazpacho 51

Curried Black Bean and Sweet Potato Soup... 47
Curried Goat Cheese Cakes 61
Curried Lentils.. 98
Curried Mashed Red Potatoes 80

Desserts. See Sweets

Drinks
Cardamom Tamarind Juice 138
Hibiscus Cooler 138
Jambo Cafe Chai 139
Mango Ginger Lemonade 137
Spiced Cinnamon Tea 137

Ethiopian Spiced Seafood Gumbo 97

Fennel
Baharat Spice Burger with Caramelized

INDEX

Fennel 109

Fish
Banana Leaf-Wrapped Island-Spiced Mahi Mahi with Tamarind Coconut Sauce 120
Ethiopian Spiced Seafood Gumbo 97
Papaya Habañero Marinated Grilled Swordfish 123
Pecan Encrusted Salmon 113
Spice Marinated Rock Fish in Corn Husks 119
White Corn Meal Encrusted Dover Sole 118

Fresh Mango and Ginger Chutney 73
Ginger Rum Sweet Potatoes 80

Guava
Spicy coconut Guava Lime Soup 54

Gluten Free
Balsamic Garlic Marinated Grilled Asparagus 82
Banana Leaf-Wrapped Island-Spiced Mahi Mahi with Tamarind Coconut Sauce 120
Cassava Fries 65
Cassava and Plantain Fufu 23
Cilantro Mango Lime Sauce 74
Cinnamon Dusted Plantains 63
Cinnamon Smoked Paprika Slow Roasted Beef Brisket 110
Coconut Basmati Rice 83
Coconut Cardamom Rice Cake 128
Coconut Goat Cheese Corn Meal 83
Coconut Rum Black Rice Pudding 131
Curried Black Bean and Sweet Potato Soup 47
Curried Lentils 98
Curried Mashed Red Potatoes 80
Ethiopian Spiced Seafood Gumbo 97
Fresh Mango and Ginger Chutney 73
Ginger Rum Sweet Potatoes 80
Goat Pilau 105
Green Mango Coconut Chutney 71
Grilled Pineapple with Vanilla Ice Cream and Honey 134
Grilled Tomatillo Spiced Mango Sauce 77
Island Spicy Peanut Coconut Chicken 89
Jambo Coconut Chicken Curry 87
Kenyan Beef Kebabs 102
Lamu Style Coconut Spinach 82
Mango Ginger Gazpacho 51
Marinated Garlic and Basil Grilled Shrimp 67
Mkate Wa Mufa 19
Mkate Wa Nazi 18
Moroccan Lamb Stew 91
Moroccan Spice Chicken Kebabs 101
Papaya Habañero Marinated Grilled Swordfish 123
Peanut Chicken Kebabs 68
Pecan Encrusted Salmon 113
Pili Pili Shrimp with Coconut Sauce 117
Pineapple Coconut Rum Chutney 75
Plantain Fried Crab Cakes 57
Ras el Hanout Chicken and Olive Stew 88
Roasted Butternut Squash and Crab Bisque 52
Roasted Ginger-Butternut Squash Bisque 48

INDEX

Sautéed Spinach with Garlic 81
Slow Cooked Beef in African Spices 95
Slow Roasted Harissa Leg of Lamb 107
Spice Marinated Rock Fish in
    Corn Husks 119
Spicy coconut Guava Lime Soup 54
Swahili Bajia 59
Swahili Shrimp Pilau 114
Sweet Smoked Paprika Corn and
    Sweet Potato Soup 49
Ugali 22
Vegetable Avocado and Corn
    Gazpacho 53
White Corn Meal Encrusted
    Dover Sole 118

Goat
Goat Pilau 105

Goat Pilau 105

Green Mango Coconut Chutney 71
Grilled Pineapple with Vanilla Ice Cream
    and Honey 134
Grilled Tomatillo Spiced Mango Sauce 77
Harissa Spice Blend 34
Slow Roasted Harissa Leg of Lamb 107
Hibiscus Cooler 138

How To
Choose a Coconut 71
Choose a Mango 73
Choose a Pineapple 75
Choose a Tomatillo 77

Make Roti 26
Open a Coconut 72
Peel Cassava Root 66

Island Spicy Peanut Coconut Chicken 89
Jambo Cafe Chai 139
Jambo Coconut Chicken Curry 87
Kenyan Beef Kebabs 102

Lamb
Moroccan Lamb Stew 91
Slow Roasted Harissa Leg of Lamb 107

Lamu Style Coconut Spinach 82

Legumes. See Beans

Mango (fruit or juice)
Banana Leaf-Wrapped Island-Spiced Mahi
    Mahi with Tamarind Coconut Sauce 120
Cilantro Mango Lime Sauce 74
Green Mango Coconut Chutney 71
Grilled tomatillo Spiced Mango Sauce 77
Fresh Mango and Ginger Chutney 73
Mango Ginger Gazpacho 51
Mango Ginger Lemonade 137
Mkate Wa Maji Stuffed with
    Tropical Fruit 133

Mango Ginger Gazpacho 51
Mango Ginger Lemonade 137
Marinated Garlic and Basil
    Grilled Shrimp 67

INDEX

Meat. See Beef, Bison, Chicken, Goat, Lamb

*Mkate Wa Maji Stuffed with
   Tropical Fruit* 133
Mkate Wa Mufa 19
Mkate Wa Nazi 18
Moroccan Lamb Stew 91
Moroccan Spice Chicken Kebabs 101

Nuts

Butter
   Island Spicy Peanut Coconut Chicken 89

Peanuts
   Peanut Chicken Kebabs 68

Pecans
   Pecan Encrusted Salmon 119

Pistachios
   Curried Goat Cheese Cakes 61
   Pistachio Crusted Curried Chicken 103

Okra
   Ethiopian Spiced Seafood Gumbo 97

Olives
   Ras El Hanout Chicken and Olive Stew 88

*Papaya Habañero Marinated Grilled
   Swordfish* 123
Peanut Chicken Kebabs 68
Pecan Encrusted Salmon 113

Peppers (Bell)
   Ethiopian Spiced Seafood Gumbo 97

Fresh Mango and Ginger Chutney 73
Mango Ginger Gazpacho 51
Ras el Hanout Chicken and Olive Stew ... 88
Swahili Shrimp Pilau 114
Vegetable Avocado and Corn Gazpacho . 53

Pili Pili Shrimp with Coconut Sauce 117

Pili Pili Spice Paste 35
   Bison Meatballs in Moroccan Spice Stew ... 93

Pineapple
   Pineapple Coconut Rum Chutney 75
   Grilled Pineapple with Vanilla Ice Cream
      and Honey 134
   Mkate Wa Maji Stuffed with
      Tropical Fruit 133

Pineapple Coconut Rum Chutney 75
Pistachio Crusted Curried Chicken 103

Plantain
Cassava and Plantain Fufu 23
Cinnamon Dusted Plantains 63
Plantain Fried Crab Cakes 57
Plantain Fried Crab Cakes 57

Potatoes

Red
   Curried Mashed Red Potatoes 80
   Goat Pilau 105
   Swahili Shrimp Pilau 114

Russet
   Spice Battered Potatoes 60

INDEX

Sweet
Bison Meatballs in Moroccan Spice
 Stew...93
Curried Black Bean and Sweet Potato
 Soup...47
Ginger Rum Sweet Potatoes......................80
Moroccan Lamb Stew....................................91
Ras El Hanout Chicken and Olive Stew......88
Roasted Butternut Squash and
 Crab Bisque...52
Sweet Smoked Paprika Corn and
 Sweet Potato Soup...................................49

Raisins
Moroccan Lamb Stew....................................91
Ras El Hanout Chicken and Olive Stew......88

Ras El Hanout Chicken and Olive Stew 88

Ras el Hanout Spice Blend............35
Ras El Hanout Chicken and Olive Stew......88

Rice
Coconut Basmati Rice....................................83
Coconut Cardamom Rice Cake................128
Coconut Rum Black Rice Pudding..........131
Goat Pilau..105
Swahili Shrimp Pilau...................................114

Rice Flour
Ethiopian Spiced Seafood Gumbo............97
Mkate Wa Nazi..18

Roasted Ginger-Butternut Squash Bisque ... 48

*Roasted Butternut Squash and
 Crab Bisque 52*
Roti 24
Sautéed Spinach with Garlic..................... 81

Sauces. See Chutneys

Seafood. See Fish, Crab, Shrimp

Shrimp
Ethiopian Spiced Seafood Gumbo............97
Marinated Garlic and Basil
 Grilled Shrimp..67
Pili Pili Shrimp with Coconut Sauce...... 117

Sides
Balsamic Garlic Marinated Grilled
 Asparagus..82
Coconut Basmati Rice....................................83
Coconut Goat Cheese Corn Meal..............83
Curried Mashed Red Potatoes...................80
Ginger Rum Sweet Potatoes......................80
Lamu Style Coconut Spinach.....................82
Sautéed Spinach with Garlic......................81

Slow Cooked Beef in African Spice Blend 95
Slow Roasted Harissa Leg of Lamb......... 107

Small Plates
Cassava Fries..65
Cinnamon Dusted Plantains......................63
Curried Goat Cheese Cakes........................61
Marinated Garlic and Basil
 Grilled Shrimp..67

INDEX

Peanut Chicken Kebabs 68
Plantain Fried Crab Cakes 57
Spice Battered Potatoes 60
Swahili Bajia 59

Soups
Curried Black Bean and Sweet Potato 47
Mango Ginger Gazpacho 51
Roasted Butternut Squash and
    Crab Bisque 52
Roasted Ginger-Butternut Squash
    Bisque 48
Spice Coconut Guava Lime Soup 54
Sweet Smoked Paprika Corn and
    Sweet Potato 49
Vegetable Avocado and Corn Gazpacho 53

Spice Battered Potatoes *60*

Spice Blends
Baharat Spice Blend 34
Harissa Spice Blend 34
Ras el Hanout Spice Blend 35
Pili Pili Spice Paste...................................... 36

Spice Marinated Rock Fish in
    Corn Husks *119*
Spiced Cinnamon Tea *137*
Spicy coconut Guava Lime Soup............... *54*

Spinach
Lamu Style Coconut Spinach..................... 82
Sautéed Spinach with Garlic 81

Squash
Butternut
    Roasted Ginger Butternut Squash
        Bisque..48
    Roasted Butternut Squash and
        Crab Bisque 52
Yellow
    Vegetable Avocado and Corn Gazpacho ...53
Zucchini
    Vegetable Avocado and Corn Gazpacho ...53

Stews
Bison Meatballs in Moroccan Spice
    Stew... 93
Curried Lentils 98
Ethiopian Spiced Seafood Gumbo 97
Jambo Coconut Chicken Curry 87
Island Spicy Peanut Coconut Chicken 89
Moroccan Lamb Stew 91
Ras El Hanout Chicken and Olive Stew ... 88
Slow Cooked Beef in African Spice
    Blend 95

Swahili Bajia.. 59
Swahili Shrimp Pilau............................. 114

Sweets
Coconut Cardamom Rice Cake 128
Coconut Chocolate Bread Pudding 129
Coconut Rum Black Rice Pudding.......... 131
Grilled Pineapple with Vanilla Ice Cream
    and Honey 134

INDEX

Mkate Wa Maji Stuffed with
Tropical Fruit.......................... 133
Vitu Vanganu with Cardamom 127

***Sweet Smoked Paprika Corn and
Sweet Potato Soup............................. 49***

Tamarind
Banana Leaf-Wrapped Island-Spiced Mahi
Mahi with Tamarind Coconut Sauce 120
Cardamom Tamarind Juice...................... 138

Tomatillos
Grilled Tomatillo Spiced Mango Sauce 77

Ugali 22
Vegetable Avocado and Corn Gazpacho 53

Vegetarian
Balsamic Garlic Marinated
Grilled Asparagus......................82
Cassava Fries............................65
Cassava and Plantain Fufu 23
Cilantro Mango Lime Sauce 74
Cinnamon Dusted Plantains..............63
Coconut Basmati Rice 83
Coconut Cardamom Rice Cake 128
Coconut Chocolate Bread Pudding....... 129
Coconut Goat Cheese Corn Meal............83
Coconut Rum Black Rice Pudding......... 131
Curried Mashed Red Potatoes.................80
Curried Black Bean and Sweet Potato
Soup 47
Curried Goat Cheese Cakes 61
Curried Lentils..............................98
Fresh Mango and Ginger Chutney...........73
Ginger Rum Sweet Potatoes...................80
Green Mango Coconut Chutney..............71
Grilled Tomatillo Spiced Mango Sauce ...77
Lamu Style Coconut Spinach...................82
Mango Ginger Gazpacho 51
Mkate Wa Maji Stuffed with
Tropical Fruit............................. 133
Mkate Wa Mufa 19
Mkate Wa Nazi 18
Pineapple Coconut Rum Chutney 75
Roasted Ginger-Butternut Squash
Bisque..48
Roti..24
Sautéed Spinach with Garlic 81
Spice Battered Potatoes 60
Spicy coconut Guava Lime Soup............54
Swahili Bajia.......................................59
Sweet Smoked Paprika Corn and
Sweet Potato Soup......................49
Ugali..22
Vegetable Avocado and Corn Gazpacho 53
Vitu Vanganu with Cardamom 127

Vitu Vanganu with Cardamom 127
White Corn Meal Encrusted Dover Sole 118

AHMED OBO

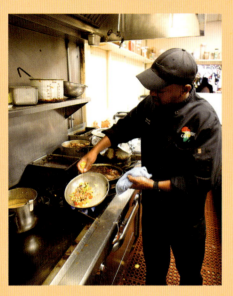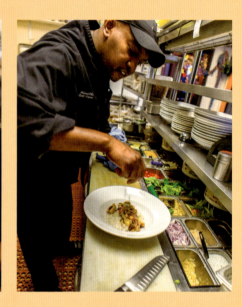

Ahmed M. Obo is the widely acclaimed founder and chef-owner of Jambo Café in Santa Fe, NM. Originally from Lamu, an island off the coast of Kenya, Ahmed came to America in 1995, worked in restaurant kitchens in Santa Fe and New York, and opened Jambo Café in August, 2009. In a city overflowing with renowned chefs and famous restaurants, Jambo has been a remarkable success. Popular with locals and families, foodies and tourists, Jambo and Chef Ahmed have been winning accolades and awards since the restaurant first opened. Starting in 2010, Ahmed won Santa Fe's *Souper Bowl* four years in a row, competing against the best chefs in the city. Jambo was voted #1 Best Ethnic/International Restaurant for five years running in the *Santa Fe Reporter's* annual "Best of Santa Fe" competition and Best Chef in Santa Fe in 2015. A beloved and admired member of the Santa Fe community, Chef Ahmed participates in events for Gerard's House, Kitchen Angels, The Food Depot, Creativity for Peace, Big Brothers/Big Sisters, St. Elizabeth's Shelter, and many more. He is an annual participant in the *Santa Fe Wine and Chile Fiesta*. In 2013, Jambo Café was featured in an episode of *Diners, Drive-Ins and Dives*. Since its opening, Jambo's customers have been clamoring for a Jambo Café Cookbook and it's finally here.